BITS OF BIOGRAPHY

or

Interesting Stories of Interesting
People

Compiled by A. L. Byers

GOSPEL TRUMPET COMPANY

Anderson, Indiana

Copyright, 1922
by
Gospel Trumpet Company

Printed in U. S. A.

CONTENTS

A Prominent Character in American History	5
Harriet Beecher Stowe	8
The Conversion of Robert Moffat	12
The Life-Story of an African Prince	15
Elizabeth Fry	19
A Noted Missionary to the South Sea Islands	23
Daniel's Purchase	27
Queen Victoria	31
Heroic Ann Judson of Burma	36
A Modern Miracle	47
Dorothea Lynde Dix	57
Margaret Fuller Ossoli	62
Some of Aunt Harriet's Experiences	67
A Great Reformer	71
Imprisoned for the Glory of God	74
The Wesleys and Their Work	77
Lincoln and His Mother	85
Lincoln's Good Qualities	90
The Helen Keller of China	93
Saint Patrick	95
The President and His Mother	96
Florence Nightingale	98
From Poverty to the Presidential Chair	105
A Blind Girl Who Became Famous	109
A Great Man Who Loved His Mother	119
Ludwig Van Beethoven	123
From Plow to Mission-Field	126
Life-Story of D. L. Moody	130
Our Own Helen Keller	137
Benjamin Franklin—A Self-Made Man	143
The Printer Boy	146
The Story of a Busy Life	148
A Missionary to the Red Man	152
Success Despite Misfortunes	156
Timid Clara's Great Success	158

BITS OF BIOGRAPHY

A PROMINENT CHARACTER IN AMERICAN HISTORY

ANDREW JACKSON was of Scotch-Irish descent. His parents had emigrated to America and settled in North Carolina. On Mar. 15, 1767, shortly after the death of his father, Andrew was born, destined to become the seventh president of the United States.

Even in boyhood days, Andrew showed strong tendencies toward leadership and military attainments. When he was but a boy of eight years, the battle of Lexington occurred, which marked the beginning of the American colonies' long struggle for independence, and Andrew manifested no little interest in the conflict. He often wished himself a man so that he, too, could fight against the enemies of his country. Finally, before the war was ended, he and his older brother, Robert, joined the army as scouts and soon afterward were taken prisoners by the English.

A scene took place between Andrew and a British officer which clearly manifested the spirit of the young soldier. "One of the Redcoat officers commanded the lads to clean his boots. They both refused. 'Sir,' said Andrew, proudly, speaking for them both, 'I am a prisoner of war, and demand to be treated as such.' 'I never heard such insolence,' fumed the British officer. 'Black those boots instantly!' 'I am not a servant to any Briton that breathes,' Andrew returned, coldly. Thoroughly infuriated, the British officer rushed upon the boy, striking at him with his sword. Instinctively Andrew raised his hand, and the blow aimed at his head cut his finger to the bone. His hand bore the scar to the end of his life."

Their mother secured the release of her sons, but two days later Robert died in her arms, of smallpox contracted in the British camps. Andrew also passed through a long illness caused by the same disease. And soon after this their brave little mother died of ship-fever caught while tending the sick on the prison-vessels at Charleston. This left Andrew an orphan at the age of sixteen, penniless and alone in this big, cold world. But this brave-spirited boy would succeed, no matter how sad or hard were the circumstances. "Difficulties are the stepping-stones to success," and this truth was clearly demonstrated in the remainder of Andrew's life. It is said of him that the secret of his success was that he always did his best.

For a time Andrew lived in the home of a distant relative and worked as a saddler. Then he taught school, and later began the study of law. Now we behold him in his upward career passing from one place of prominence to another—public prosecutor of the western part of North Carolina which later became the State of Tennessee, representative in Congress, a United States senator, judge of the Supreme Court, Mayor-General, and, before becoming president of the United States in 1829, he served his country in the Creek Indian War, where he won the name "Old Hickory," and in the War of 1812, being the hero of the famous battle of New Orleans.

In 1791 Andrew Jackson was married to Rachel Robards, of Nashville, Tenn., and "it is said that history does not record a happier marriage. To the world he was overbearing and harsh, and was often profane;

but with her he was patient, gentle, and courteous, and when he won renown, she was happy for his sake." Thus we have a glimpse of the noble side, as well as a disparaging view, of this great man's character. Jackson had a fiery temper, which made for him many enemies; but while he had his passions and stood defiantly against those who opposed him, yet his feelings for women and children or the weak and helpless were those of protection and support.

On Dec. 23, 1824, "Rachel, his beloved wife, died, leaving her husband utterly stunned and broken-hearted over his loss. For years he was inconsolable, and until the end of his life he wore her picture upon a chain about his neck. There was no other woman in the world for him. When he came to the presidency in 1829, he provided the White House with no mistress, and during his eight years of residence there the gentle face of his wife was the last thing upon which Jackson looked at night. It was the first thing upon which his eyes rested in the morning."

At the close of his second term as president, he retired, in his seventieth year, to his home—The Hermitage—near Nashville, where he passed the remaining eight years of his life, always, however, manifesting a deep interest in public affairs.

HARRIET BEECHER STOWE

"DO YOU think you can have all that and heaven too?" said a deacon as he stood at the door-step of Dr. Lyman Beecher's parsonage, and actually beheld a beautiful carpet on the floor. In reality, though, the carpet was made only of cotton cloth, neatly designed and painted by the parson's skilful wife. At that time small salaries and large families was the rule for ministers, and Doctor Beecher was no exception, he was the father of thirteen children. Harriet was the seventh of the family, and in her early childhood she learned something about poverty. But to her, poverty was a wise schoolmaster, for the hardships she had to endure brought out the best that was in her character. Besides, she became accomplished in various domestic duties. At the age of eight she could sew and knit well. She also darned the family stockings. Although Harriet enjoyed quiet domestic duties, she was full of life and found delight in ranging the fields and forests.

When Harriet was between three and four years old her mother died, so her personal recollections of Mother were few. Nevertheless, Harriet was greatly influenced by her mother's godly example, for she was continually hearing some one mention some incident in her life. From what she heard from others, Harriet learned that her mother was a woman of strong faith and prevailing prayer. One example is that she prayed that her sons might devote themselves to the ministry. This prayer was answered, for all her sons became converted and entered that calling.

An example of Mrs. Beecher's patience is shown by the following incident: One day while she was absent the children found a package of what they called onions. Harriet felt sure that they were real onions and good to eat, though her brother had his doubts. They proceeded to eat them, and just as they had finished the last one the mother appeared. Upon finding that

Home of Harriet Beecher Stowe, Hartford, Conn.

the children had devoured a package of choice tulip bulbs that her brother had sent her from New York, she did not scold, but told them how sorry she felt and that if they had left them they would have had some beautiful flowers. Her attitude had more effect upon the children than any punishment could have had.

About a year after Harriet's mother died, a stepmother entered the home and filled her place as well as any woman could.

Meaningless conversation was not allowed in the

Beecher home. The table-talk was in itself a good school. Books, authors, character, and religion were freely discussed. The children were taught to value books, and when a new one was brought into the home it was first read aloud, and later read by the different members of the family individually. Harriet loved to slip away into her father's library, where she looked over his books and sermons and wondered if she would ever be able to understand them. At an early age she began writing down her thoughts, and at the age of ten she wrote excellent compositions in school. When she was twelve years old her composition on Can the Immortality of the Soul Be Proved by the Light of Nature? was read at an annual school entertainment.

At the age of fourteen Harriet attended a girls' school at Hartford, Conn., conducted by her sister. In a few months she was able to assist her sister in teaching.

About this time, one Sunday morning, as she listened to her father's sermon telling of Christ as a friend, she was touched by the Savior's love and gave her heart to him.

The family soon moved to Boston, where Harriet continued her studies. Six years later, when her father was called to the presidency of the Lane Theological Seminary, of Cincinnati, Ohio, he took Harriet and her sister with him to what was then a new country. There the two daughters established the Western Female Institution and became successful teachers. It was not long until Harriet was married to the Rev. Calvin E. Stowe, a professor in the theological school. His salary was small, and the lessons in economy Harriet had learned during her childhood were a great help to her in rearing her family of six children. She was a devoted mother, and the care of her family prevented her giving much time to writing. Nevertheless she did some writing and thereby helped her husband support the family.

During her life in Cincinnati, on the border of a slave State, Mrs. Stowe learned much about slavery. In Cincinnati the opposition to slavery was hot, while across the Ohio River in Kentucky the pro-slavery sentiment was equally violent. The things she saw and heard here so aroused her soul that when, soon after, she moved to a quiet country home near Brunswick, Me., she wrote the most remarkable book of the nineteenth century, a book that was one of the greatest factors in abolishing slavery—Uncle Tom's Cabin. Many of the characters of this book were people with whom she was personally acquainted during her life in Cincinnati. The publication of this book brought Mrs. Stowe great popularity, as well as a comfortable living. Besides its wide circulation in America and England, it was published in all the European languages. When at last the slaves were freed, Mrs. Stowe felt that this alone more than rewarded her for all her labor and sacrifice. She did not claim to be the author of the book, but only a humble instrument in God's hands in the production of it.

During twenty-six years of her life Mrs. Stowe produced twenty-three volumes, besides a large number of articles for magazines. Each book was written for the purpose of uplifting humanity, either in a domestic, social, intellectual, or religious way.

THE CONVERSION OF ROBERT MOFFAT

NEAR the age of sixteen, after working about a year in a nursery-garden near his home at Ormiston, East Lothian, Scotland, Robert Moffat was called to fill a responsible position in Cheshire, England. The day came when he had to say farewell to his dear home folks. His mother proposed going with him to the boat that was to take him across the River Forth. His heart was glad with the thought of obtaining a better position, but he could not help showing some emotion at parting, because he thought perhaps they would never meet again in this world.

As they drew near to the spot where they were to part, his mother said, "Now, my Robert, let us stand here for a few minutes, for I wish to ask one favor of you before we part, and I know you will not refuse to do what your mother asks."

"What is it, Mother?" Robert inquired.

"Do promise me first that you will do what I ask, and I shall tell you."

"No, Mother, I can not till you tell me what your wish is."

"O Robert, can you think for a moment that I shall ask you, my son, to do anything that is not right? Do not I love you?"

"Yes, Mother, I know you do, but I do not like to make promises that I may not be able to fulfil."

Robert kept his eyes fixed on the ground. He was trying to resist his feelings of emotion. His mother sighed deeply, which made him look up into her face. He saw the tears roll down her dear cheeks and was conquered at once. And as soon as he could speak he cried out, "O Mother, ask what you will and I will do it."

CONVERSION OF ROBERT MOFFAT

She replied, "I only ask whether you will read a chapter in the Bible every morning and another every evening?"

"Mother," spoke up Robert, "you know I read my Bible."

"I know you do. But you do not read it regularly, or as a duty you owe to God, its Author. And," she added, "now I shall return home with a happy heart, inasmuch as you have promised to read the Scriptures daily. O Robert, my son, read much in the New Testament. Read much in the Gospels—the blessed Gospels. Then you can not well go astray. If you pray, the Lord himself will teach you."

Robert parted from his mother and was soon among strangers. He was a strong boy, full of physical and mental energy, but it required all this to keep up with his new responsibilities. He had very little time to himself. He lived far from any religious services and had to mingle with the gay and thoughtless, but he never forgot his promise to his mother.

He read chiefly in the New Testament, at first as a pleasing duty he owed to his mother, but in doing this he became familiar with the Gospels.

After a while he became uneasy, then unhappy. Many times while busy at work this question would be thrust upon him, "What think ye of Christ?" He wished he could cease reading the Bible, but the thought of his mother and the promise he had made held him to continue. He felt wretched, but still did not pray. He tried hard to stifle conviction.

One night he arose in a state of terror from a frightful dream. He fell on his knees before God, feeling as if his sins were tumbling down upon him like a great mountain. Then began a struggle between hope and despair. For weeks he was miserable. He wished to feel that he was converted, but he could not.

He resolved to become as wicked as he could so that if he ever should be converted the change would be so evident that he could not doubt it. Then he considered the awful leap he was about to make and trembled at the thought that he might perish in his sins. He knew of no one to whom he could pour out the agony that burned within him. He tried to pray, but thought there was a black cloud between him and God.

He lived alone in a little lodge in an extensive garden and had a little time he could call his own. One evening he was poring over the Epistle to the Romans. He had read these same passages many times before, but this evening they seemed altogether different. With a heart nearly broken, he cried out, "Can it be possible that I have never understood what I have been reading?" He kept turning from one passage to another, each one sending new light into his darkened soul. The truths of salvation were revealed to him. He saw what God had done for the sinner and what the sinner must do to obtain the favor of God and be assured of eternal life. His struggles were at an end. He now realized that, being justified by faith, he had peace with God.

He had undergone a great change of heart, and this, he said, was produced by the Spirit of God through the reading of the Bible.

With all the energy of which he was capable, Robert Moffat threw himself into the work of the Lord. His leisure time was spent in the study of the Bible, and whenever he could, he was trying to convince others of their need of salvation. About a year from this time the Lord called him to Africa as a missionary.

THE LIFE-STORY OF AN AFRICAN PRINCE

ABOUT midway down the west coast of Africa lies the little coffee-producing country of Liberia. Far back from the coast opposite Cape Palms was the home of Sammy, a little colored boy with the thick lips and flat nose that unmistakably proclaimed him a negro through and through. His father was one of the petty kings of that country who ruled over such heathen subjects as resorted to them for companionship or protection. The relationship among these tribal peoples was not always the most friendly, and there were frequent uprisings and fierce struggles. In one such Sammy was torn from home and mother and taken prisoner. A second time he was kidnapped and carried away. His father offered Sammy's baby sister as the ransom, but Sammy, thinking himself more able than she to endure the hardships of slavery, pled with his father not to make the bargain.

Sammy's captor, enraged at not being able to obtain the price he had set for the release of the boy, began whipping him. Daily that savage master laid stripes upon the bare back of the little prisoner. At last Sammy decided he could endure it no longer. One day while his cruel master was whipping him with a rope-like vine, Sammy ran from under the lash and into the woods, not knowing where he should go. But after many days of weary travel he reached the coast and secured work on a coffee plantation. Sammy was then a little more than eleven years old.

Just how long he remained on the plantation, we know not, but some wonderful changes were there wrought in his life. He learned to speak English, and to read and write a little, and was converted.

The first time Sammy was taken inside a church-building he could not understand what he saw and heard,

An African prince—Sammy Morris

but he felt a presence pure and, to him, awful. From this Sammy could not get away. He felt himself so unclean. His agony of soul caused him to pray at very unseasonable hours, and his companions, often disturbed in their slumbers by his cries, declared that if Sammy could not behave himself better he must leave the quarters. So Sammy moved his prayer-meeting to the woods.

One night after one of his midnight meetings he returned to the quarters for rest, but he could not sleep. His heart, he said, kept praying. Suddenly his room grew light, then lighter, until it was filled with glory. At first Sammy thought it must be the sun rising, but as he beheld his companions soundly sleeping he decided it must be God. Presently his burden disappeared, and he began to leap and shout and praise God. There was no more sleep in the camp that night. Some thought Sammy had gone crazy, and others thought a devil had gotten into him.

Not long afterward, the newly converted boy felt it his duty to preach the gospel to his people. But on confiding his burden to a missionary friend he was informed that to preach he must be educated, and that to be educated he must go to America. To do this would take money, and Sammy had not a single cent. But he knew on whom to call for it. He hastened to the woods to "talk to his Father," as he called praying. He related his needs to God in sentence after sentence and plead with him to supply them, and in after-years when he rehearsed the incident, he said, "I knew he would."

Twice he approached the captain of a ship for passage to America, but each time met with cuffs, curses, and kicks. Nothing daunted, he approached the captain the third time, and secured passage as a workman. His ignorance brought him much trouble, but his peace of soul was indescribable.

He soon found he did not need to wait for an education in order to win souls. One morning when he went in to clean up the cabin the captain was converted, and before the ship reached New York more than half the crew had been saved. The first night he was in New York City he entered a mission to wait for a man who was to provide him a place to stay. When the man returned, Sammy was standing on the platform with seventeen men on their faces around him. He had just pointed them to Jesus, and they were rejoicing. That was on Friday. On Sunday he was taken to Sunday-school and asked to speak. He had scarcely begun when the altar was filled with young people weeping and sobbing. These works were wrought by an uncultured, uncouth, uncultivated African, but his strength was in his life of prayer. His very presence and his very touch seemed to bring one in contact with God.

A short time later he entered an Indiana university to prepare for what he considered his life-work. His ambition was to devote himself to the children of his race. He often said, "When I get back to Africa I will gather the children about me and they will sit on the sand. They will call me father, but I won't care for that. I will tell them of Jesus, and soon some of them will go away in the bushes, and I will know what that means. When they come back they will be very happy." But his desire, only as it has been carried out by others, was never realized. A rigorous climate was too much for one who had come from a region where snow was not known. He contracted a cold, from which he never recovered. But he bore his sickness patiently. Of his desired work he said, "Others can do it better." Among his last words were, "Oh, I am so happy. I have seen the angels, and they will soon come for me." He was buried in the vast cemetery at Ft. Wayne, Ind., and perhaps no grave there has more visitors or is watered with so many tears as that of Sammy Morris.

At a prayer-meeting held shortly after his death three young men consecrated themselves to go to Africa in Sammy's stead.

ELIZABETH FRY

THAT it is in the power of woman to accomplish great things in the world, though she be a frail vessel, could not be more clearly exemplified than by the life-story of Elizabeth Fry. As a child she was frail and nervous and much afraid of the dark. Her father, thinking to remove this fear, made her go to bed in the dark, but the shock to her nervous system was so great that never in all her sixty-five years of life did she fully recover.

Elizabeth was not fond of books, but she was greatly attached to her mother, so much so that she was harassed by the thought that her mother might die. While her mother napped, Elizabeth would sit and keep watch, fearful that her mother would never awake. At the age of twelve this dreaded calamity came to her, for her mother died; but the pleasures of life wore away the affliction rapidly.

Up to this time Elizabeth had been under the strict supervision of a Quaker father and mother. The Bible was the standard of conduct in the home, and Elizabeth was expected to read it daily. But on being bereft of her mother, Elizabeth gave more attention to dress and ornamentation, and even engaged in dancing. But at the age of seventeen she came to herself, and these words are found recorded in her diary: "I am determined that I will overcome my wicked inclinations. I must not flirt; I must not be out of temper with the children; I must not contradict without a cause; I must not allow myself to be angry; I must not exaggerate, which I am inclined to do; I must not give way to luxury; I must not be idle in mind; I must try to give way to every good feeling, and overcome every bad. I have lately been satirical, so as to hurt sometimes; remember it is a fault to hurt others. If I had religion, I should be superior to what I am. I think I am by degrees losing many excellent qualities. I am more cross, more proud, more vain, more extravagant. I lay it to my great love of gaiety and the world. I feel, I know, I am falling.''

Just about the time Elizabeth was having this battle with herself, an eminent Quaker preacher arrived at Norwich, England, Elizabeth's home, to hold a meeting. Elizabeth and her six sisters, dressed in clothes by no means after the plain Quaker style, attended, and sat together. The message delivered was, it seems, especially suited to Elizabeth. The tone of the speaker was melodious and tender, and secured Elizabeth's undivided attention. Before the service was half over, Elizabeth was in tears over her sins, and on the way home in the carriage she gave full vent to her feelings in convulsive sobs.

The next day the minister visited her, and from that day her love of the world and worldly pleasures seemed gone. How she was changed is shown by the following taken from her diary: ''Today I have felt that there is a God! I have been devotional, and my mind has been led away from the follies that it is mostly wrapped up in. We had much serious conversation; in short, what he said, and what I felt, was like a refreshing shower falling upon earth that had been dried for ages. It has not made me unhappy; I have felt ever since *humble*. I have longed for virtue; I hope to be truly virtuous; to let sophistry fly from my mind; not to be enthusiastic and foolish, but only to be so far religious as will lead to virtue.''

ELIZABETH FRY

For a time she had severe battles, but one night she had a dream that brought to her soul the consciousness of real faith. At once she donned the "close cap and plain kerchief of a Quakeress," and consecrated herself to works of charity by opening a school for poor children who roamed the streets with none to care for them.

Shortly after this, she married, but the duties of married life interfered little with her other work. Her home was a house of entertainment to Friends from all parts of the country. And she began as soon as possible to minister to the needs of London's slum inhabitants.

In 1809 her father died, and a few minutes after his death she knelt beside the bed on which the dead loved one lay and reconsecrated herself to the service of God. From that time she was a minister and became engaged in the work for which she is most known—prison reform. She entered places into which others except officers were afraid to go. But with a heart of love burdened with a message for the fallen she knew no defeat. Success was hers, and in a short time she became the most famous woman in England. Her magical influence over the most hardened prisoners interested even the Queen. Honors were heaped upon her in abundance, not only by those of her own country, but by those of many countries.

The last communication she wrote was addressed to a society in charge of philanthropic work, and it read as follows: "My much beloved friends, amidst many sorrows that have been permitted for me to pass through, and much bodily suffering, I still feel a deep and lively interest in the cause of poor prisoners, and earnest is my prayer that the God of all grace may be very near to help you to be stedfast in the important Christian work of seeking to win the poor wanderers to return, repent, and live."

On October 13, 1845, after a few hours of intense bodily suffering, Elizabeth Fry suddenly and triumphantly passed out of this life to receive her crown.

A NOTED MISSIONARY TO THE SOUTH SEA ISLANDS

A YOUNG man of perhaps eighteen years stood one evening on a certain street in London. He was impatiently awaiting a friend who had agreed to meet him there. At length, a lady, the wife of his employer, approached him and asked that he go with her to a meeting in Whitefield Tabernacle near by. He declined, explaining to her why he must remain. She was not satisfied, however, and continued to urge him. He finally yielded and accompanied her to the meeting.

This proved to be the turning-point in that young man's life, for during the sermon conviction fastened itself upon him so strongly that then and there he gave his heart to God. This young man was John Williams. He was born in 1796, in a little house on the brow of a hill in Tottenham, then six miles from London. As a child, he was characterized by a sunny, affectionate disposition, which won for him many friends. His mother was a Christian woman, and every day she would gather her children about her to teach them and pray with them. John thought religion too gloomy for an active young person like himself, so he lived a very worldly, though moral, life up until the evening of his conversion.

Soon after this memorable evening, John Williams began his Christian work as a Sunday-school teacher, a visitor among the sick, and a distributer of tracts. This was but the beginning of loving, self-sacrificing service to God, which continued throughout his life.

As time passed, a conviction grew upon Mr. Williams that God wanted him to go as a missionary to the South

Sea islands. In November, 1816, just a month after his marriage, he and his wife left for Sydney, Australia, and just one year from that time they landed at Tahiti, one of the islands of Polynesia. In ten months Mr. Williams had learned the language and was preaching to the copper-colored natives about the Savior, who had died that they might be saved. He soon won many friends, and, as a result, there was a great interest manifested in the gospel. In the first baptismal service seventy persons professed their faith in Christ as their personal Savior.

Mr. Williams would remain long enough on one island to build a place of worship and establish Christianity, and then he would go on to another. While on the Island of Raiatia, where God abundantly blessed his labors, he received the sad news of his mother's death. He felt grieved the more because his father was yet unsaved. He wrote an affectionate letter to him, pleading with him to give his heart to God. Seven years later, his father's last words were: "The father is saved through the son's pleading."

Many islands were visited in succession, and, with the aid of helpers, he established the gospel in many of them. Wonderful were the changes that took place as a result of the introduction of Christianity. Idolatry was destroyed, wars were stopped, sanitary conditions were introduced, and a long list of marvelous transformations took place in the lives of the natives as soon as they learned to know and serve the Lord Jesus Christ.

When the party sailed for the Samoa Islands, Fauea, one of the chiefs, who had been converted some time before that, was with them. On landing, they were surrounded by the natives, who flocked to them. And Fauea explained to the natives about the wonderful

MISSIONARY TO SOUTH SEA ISLANDS 25

The death of John Williams

gospel the white men were bringing to them. They were all very much interested, especially in the white man's costume. One interested and inquisitive native pulled off one of Mr. Williams' shoes, and, on seeing the stocking, told Fauea very excitedly that the white man had no toes as they did. Fauea explained to him that the white men did have toes, but that they wore a covering over them. Their stay here was short but profitable. They next went to Raratonga, where, in 1834, idol-worship was completely destroyed, and all the people became professors of Christianity.

After eighteen years of faithful labors in the South Sea islands, Mr. Williams returned to England. But he was not there long before he again left for the Samoa Islands. When the ship landed, he and three others went ashore alone. They observed that the natives acted very queerly. Very soon natives rushed out from all sides, and Mr. Williams was beaten down and thrust through with arrows.

Great was the sorrow among the Christian isles of the Pacific as news was received of the death of their beloved John Williams. Pathetic was the cry of the natives everywhere: "Our father! Our father! He has turned his face from us! We shall never see him more. He that brought us the good word of salvation is gone!"

DANIEL'S PURCHASE

ONE late autumn day more than a century and a quarter ago, about the time Washington was serving his first term as President of the United States, two boys were sent from their home, a country farmhouse in a frontier New Hampshire town, to buy some groceries at the store at the "Corner," about a mile distant.

Neither of the boys was over ten, and the younger, a slight, delicate-looking lad with black hair and eyes and a swarthy complexion, was but eight years old. They were the sons of a thrifty farmer who had been a soldier of the Revolution and had taken up a rocky farm in this distant township after the war was over.

The store at the "Corner" was a small affair kept by a man named Hoyt, who combined the offices of storekeeper and pedagog in the small rural community. The school session occupied about two months and a half in the winter season, and was kept in a corner of the store, and the two lads had both been pupils of Master Hoyt. The boys entered the store, where they found Master Hoyt, a tall man of severe aspect, waiting upon a customer. But his quick eye noticed them at once.

"Good-morning, Ezekiel; good-morning, Daniel. How's the squire today?" Mr. Hoyt inquired cordially, for the boys' father was an influential man in that section and one of his best customers.

The boys answered respectfully, and after a time made their purchases; then, as they were in no hurry to go home, they spent a few minutes looking over the array of merchandise in the store. Master Hoyt, who regarded them more as pupils than customers, meanwhile kept up a stream of talk.

"I suppose you are keeping up your reading and writing, Daniel?" he said. "You must not forget what you learned last winter. You're a better reader than writer. I am afraid you'll have to get Ezekiel to set your copy when you are old enough to teach school."

"No, I don't like writing," admitted the boy with the big black eyes. "But I could always read, at least I don't remember when I was not able to read a chapter in the Bible. My mother taught me, sir."

"Your mother's a smart and an educated woman, and your father's a smart man, though his education is not anything to brag about. I hope, Daniel, you'll grow up to be a smart man, too. What'll you be? A farmer, I suppose."

The boy murmured somewhat indistinctly that he did not think he should like farming, and the trader saw that he had his eyes fixed on an article displayed on a line hung over the counter. It was a cotton handkerchief that was nearly all covered with printed letters.

"Oh, I see that you take a fancy to that pocket-handkerchief. Would you like to look at it, Daniel?"

"Yes, sir, I would. Is that a story printed on it?"

"No, it's the Constitution of the United States, my boy," said Master Hoyt, as he placed the flimsy fabric in the lad's hands.

Daniel's interest was aroused. He did not know just what the Constitution was, but he thought he would like to know something about it.

"What is the price?" he asked.

"Twenty-five cents," was the answer.

He had just that sum in his pocket, the hard earnings and the economical savings of many months, and he took it out and looked at it. It represented his total wealth, and he had been hoarding it for another pur-

DANIEL'S PURCHASE

pose. But the temptation was too strong, and he passed his money over to the merchant and received the handkerchief in exchange.

"You have made a wise purchase, Daniel," said Master Hoyt, approvingly. "Take it home and study it, and you will learn something of the government under which we live. It's a great country, Daniel, and I hope you'll live to see it still greater."

Daniel went home with his precious handkerchief safely tucked in his pocket. He was not quite sure that he had made a wise investment, but someway the handkerchief fascinated him. He had no time to study it during the day, for he was busy doing chores about the farm; but when evening came and the family gathered about the blaze of the wide, open fireplace, he brought out his new possession and began to read it over, lying at full length on the hearth in front of the burning logs.

"What have you there, Daniel?" asked his father, observing the boy's studiousness.

"It is the Constitution of the United States printed on a handkerchief."

"Where did you get it?"

"At William Hoyt's store this morning."

"Dan spent all the money he had for it," said his brother Ezekiel.

"Well, it wasn't a bad trade, I guess," replied the squire. "It will do you no harm to be acquainted with the Constitution of your country."

His father's quiet approval was a great relief to the boy, who devoted the rest of the evening and several evenings afterward to making himself familiar with the document, of which, in future years he was destined to become so staunch and eloquent a defender and supporter. For this farmer boy, nurtured amid New Hampshire's rocks and sterile soil, and who conned his earliest lessons by the roaring blaze of his father's kitchen fireplace, lived to rank among America's greatest sons; member of Congress, Senator, Cabinet minister, and candidate for President, he is best known as the great expounder of the Constitution of the United States—Daniel Webster.

QUEEN VICTORIA

EVEN in royalty a good mother has more to do than has most anything else in the making of a great and good man or woman. This is especially true in the making of Queen Victoria, of England. Her mother, the Duchess of Kent, was talented, highly educated, and refined, but her good common sense was worth more than all these other qualities in training the little queen to be. The Duchess cared nothing for the show of royalty; she felt it was more important that her country have a modest, useful, Christian queen than a brilliant, irresponsible one. She had made a careful study of child-training, and, though she met with much opposition and criticism among her royal relatives, she held firmly to her views and put them into practise.

Victoria's father, the Duke of Kent, was the son of King George III. Her mother's brother, Leopold, King of Belgium, married Princess Charlotte, daughter of King George IV of England. She was a lady of fine character and accomplishments and the people of England looked forward with great anticipation to her reign, but she did not live long after her marriage. Another cousin of Victoria's, who was next in line in succession to the throne, died in her infancy. So it seems that a wise Providence reserved the throne for Victoria, England's best and wisest queen.

When Victoria was still a baby, her father died. This was a great sorrow to the mother, who, besides being left alone to train the young Queen, was left poor and in debt. However, her brother Leopold came to her assistance so that she was able to educate her daughter as she wished. She did not pay her husband's debts, but

Victoria, feeling that it was her sacred duty, paid them as soon as she became Queen.

No doubt the simplicity enforced upon the young Queen by poverty had much to do in the making of her character, as well as in the developing of her physically. Her mother gave much attention to the child's health. Her food was simple, and she had regular hours for eating and sleeping, with which nothing was allowed to interfere.

The regular daily routine, which was adhered to rigidly, was as follows: Breakfast of bread and milk and fruit at eight; after breakfast, an hour's walk or drive; from ten to twelve, instruction by her mother; the next two hours were spent in play, after which she had her plain dinner; the rest of the afternoon until four was occupied with her lessons, after which she went for a visit or a drive; then she had a walk or donkey-ride through the gardens; after this she had supper, then played with her nurse till bedtime, which was at nine. Even when she was sixteen years old, when a party was given her by the King and Queen, she left the festivities and retired at nine.

Though Victoria had a nurse and a governess, she was under the direct care of her mother; she had her bed beside her mother's, ate at a little table at her mother's side, and was never away from her for any long period of time. The careful attention given the child's health by her mother was rewarded by a ripe and vigorous old age.

Victoria had a small regular allowance of spending-money every month, and was taught to spend it wisely. Once on seeing in a shop-window a doll she very much desired, but not having money enough to pay for it, she asked the merchant to keep it for her till she got her next allowance. This he willingly did, and when she received the money she hurried to the shop and made her purchase.

It seems that every detail of her character was given careful attention and training. Nervous excitement, fright over dogs and spiders, etc., were not allowed, as they were thought to be below the dignity of a queen. She was very modest in her dress and manners, and in conversation seldom made any reference to royalty. She was taught to be kind to all—servants and playmates, and even to dumb animals. She was especially sympathetic toward the poor and suffering. That she still retained this tender, sympathetic disposition after she became Queen, is shown by the fact that in dealing with prisoners she would pardon them whenever possible and would not tolerate unjust punishment.

While Victoria was given time for recreation, she was not allowed to waste time. Every moment was to be profitably spent. She was taught to help herself whenever possible and not make unnecessary use of the servants. She cared for her own wardrobe and even made some repairs on her clothes. She was also taught to do some housework and cooking.

In her studies the young girl made rapid progress. She studied law, politics, and other branches that were not usually taken by wealthy English women. She also gave much attention to languages. While her education was mostly practical, she did not neglect the various arts. She learned to play and sing well, also to paint.

Nothing was said to Victoria by her mother or governess about her becoming queen until she was twelve years old. Then on a certain occasion a genealogical table was placed in a book she was reading. Upon examination of this table she found she was nearer the throne than she had thought. She did not feel like boasting, but for a time cried much over the great responsibility awaiting her.

When she was only eighteen, her uncle, King George IV, died suddenly, and when the Archbishop of Canterbury and the Lord Chamberlain came to greet her as Queen, she burst into tears and begged the Archbishop to pray for her. This shows how sensibly she felt the burden. After these officials had left, she immediately sat down and wrote a note of sympathy to her aunt, still addressing her as "Her Majesty the Queen." Next day, when Victoria was to be proclaimed Queen from a certain window of St. James Palace, appearing there in simple garb before the great throng, she was so overcome with emotion that she again burst into tears. With her mother, she took possession first of Buckingham Palace and later of Windsor Castle, and began at once to be loved by her subjects. Her first speech before Parliament was made with such a clear, strong voice and attended by such a calm bearing that her listeners were amazed.

June 28, 1838, one month after her nineteenth birthday, Queen Victoria's coronation took place, and was attended by unusual display and demonstration on the part of her subjects. The ceremony was an ancient one, and had Victoria modified it to suit her tastes she would have made a number of changes, but not wishing to be too exacting, she made only two. The first was in regard to the rule by which all bishops, archbishops, and peers, young and old (of whom there were about six hundred), were to kiss the Queen's left cheek. This was confined to two of her relatives. The other was in regard to the custom for an armored knight to appear and challenge her enemies to mortal combat. This part of the

QUEEN VICTORIA 35

ceremony was dispensed with. The old crown that had been worn by George and William, but which had been remodeled and reduced in size, was brought out and placed upon Victoria's head. Its value was $583,800. The whole ceremony was wonderful and inspiring, and the procession from Westminster Abbey to the Queen's palace was witnessed by a great cheering crowd of loving subjects.

In less than two years after her coronation Victoria was married to her cousin, Prince Albert. He was a noble young man and was much beloved by the English people. Dec. 14, 1861, he died, leaving nine children. This, together with the death of her mother the same year, was a great sorrow to Queen Victoria.

In 1901, after a long and prosperous reign, and after having endeared herself to her people and to all mankind, Queen Victoria died at the ripe old age of eighty-two years.

HEROIC ANN JUDSON OF BURMA
Part I

ANN HASSELTINE was a beautiful, graceful girl, very gay and mirthful, fond of society, and possessed of an ardent spirit and a brilliant mind. She lived in very comfortable circumstances at her home in Bradford, Mass. At the age of sixteen she was converted, and her natural ardor from that time found expression in Christian endeavor. She taught school for some years and had much longing to bring her pupils to Christ.

She first met Mr. Judson at her own home on a day when he and others were invited there to dinner. While she waited on the table she was much attracted by this excellent young man, but felt somewhat disappointed because he appeared to be entirely engrossed with his plate and paid no attention to her. She afterward learned, however, that at that very time he was composing a graceful stanza in her praise. He had already decided to go as a missionary to India; and when he offered her his hand, he spoke freely of the probable sufferings and privations of a missionary life, and asked her if for the love of Christ she was willing to share such a life with him. After much prayer and considering whether she was worthy of such a responsible position, she gave her consent, and they were married in February, 1812, when she was twenty-two. Mr. Judson was one year her senior.

They left at once for India, but Burma turned out to be their final destination. There were few foreign missionaries in those days, and most persons had little sympathy with the idea of hazarding one's life among the heathen. The young Judson couple, however,

HEROIC ANN JUDSON OF BURMA 37

would not be turned from their purpose by any discouraging remarks, but went forth fervent in spirit and strong in faith. They were the first missionaries to set sail from America, and noble examples they proved themselves to all who should follow them.

Instead of being only ten days or a month on their way to their field of labor, they were a year and a half. This was not due, however, to the slow means of travel altogether. When they arrived in India, they found the English East India Company unfavorable to missions, especially to American missionaries, for England and America were not on friendly terms then. They were in India but a few months when they were ordered to leave for England. They could not bear the thoughts of returning home, and after much difficulty got permission to go to Mauritius, an English island east of Madagascar. After a brief interval they went to Madras, India. Here again the East India Company ordered their departure within a certain time. They had to choose between returning home and going to Rangoon, Burma, for only such ships were leaving within the specified time. How strange and severe at times, and yet how faultless, are the leadings of the Divine Hand! God had a great work in Burma for this young, gifted couple and closed up other ways. To Rangoon they went, a long, tedious voyage, on which Mrs. Judson came very near losing her life.

That first evening when they lay in the Rangoon harbor their feelings were gloomy enough. It was a miserable-looking place with no trace of Western civilization, and it was in a land ruled by a cruel, heathen king whose word alone could set a man free or send him to the executioner.

When they became settled in their new home, they

Monument erected to the memory of Washington's mother

HEROIC ANN JUDSON OF BURMA

gave themselves diligently to the study of the language and the people. They often felt very lonely in that faraway land, with no society, and as yet no results of their labor. But they would entertain no thought of returning to New England to have a pleasant home and pleasant associations there. Instead of mourning over their privations, they thought of how much more comfortable was their home than most of the natives' homes and of how great their spiritual blessings while the poor people about them were in darkness. For the sake of the salvation of these poor souls they would gladly give their lives, suffering along the way whatever should fall to their lot. Mrs. Judson, instead of tempting her husband to go back or to give her an easier time, stood by his side and marched bravely with him through toil and hardship.

The baby boy who came to them when they had been there about two years brightened their lonely home, only to leave it after a few months more lonely than before. The sad mother could not be comforted, but would go to his grave and sit there for hours weeping. Yet in her heart she believed God's way best.

Not long after this sorrow, her husband, having applied himself so closely to his studies and translations, found it necessary on account of failing health to have a change. He planned a sea voyage to another part of the country and expected to be gone three months. What he suffered of disappointment, privation, and sickness on that trip would make a long chapter, but Mrs. Judson knew not of it. She waited from Christmas until the following July without tidings of him, and she knew not if he were living or dead.

During his absence a storm of persecution arose, and the other missionaries who had joined the Judsons thought it advisable to leave the country. Mrs. Judson was hardly persuaded to join them. Her heart had no rest as she floated down the river and thought of her husband's disappointment, should he arrive and find the mission broken up and her gone. She would return. In a small boat the captain provided for her she ascended the river, alone with her luggage, facing dangers and uncertainties, but calm in her heart. Not long after this her husband returned, and they were able to work a few more years without suffering violence, though their work was hindered by the government.

The strangeness, the strain, and the climate so wore on Mrs. Judson's health that nine years after her leaving America it was necessary that she return. She was absent from her husband two years and three months, and in this time her health so much improved that when Mr. Judson saw her again, he exclaimed, "This is the Ann Hasseltine of other days."

Soon after her return, she, with her husband, left the precious converts in Rangoon in the care of some other missionaries and went to Ava, the capital, to start a mission there; for the Emperor had shown them favor in various ways and given them some ground on which to build a mission house.

Part II

MR. AND MRS. JUDSON had only fairly begun their work of preaching and teaching in Ava when a new trouble arose—a trouble greater than they had ever known before. War was declared between the Burmese and the English, and all foreigners in Burma were suspected as spies. The ignorant Burmese could not appreciate the difference between an American and an Englishman.

One day when Mr. and Mrs. Judson were just ready for dinner, a dozen Burmese officers sprang in, asked for the teacher, and told him he was summoned by the king. Then one of the officers, whom they knew by his spotted face to be an executioner, threw Mr. Judson on the floor and began to bind him. Mrs. Judson hastily brought some money and offered it to the brutal man, begging him to have mercy. But there was no mercy. The cords were only drawn the tighter and Judson was dragged from her sight, she knew not whither. Nor could she follow, for a guard kept her a prisoner at the house. There was no sleep for her that night as she worried about her husband and heard the constant threatenings and diabolical language of the guard outside. The next morning she sent a servant to learn, if possible, something of her husband, and he returned with the sad news that the teacher was in the death-prison. In a few days she obtained her freedom, and then for months she worked with the utmost diligence and bravery for the release of her husband. Sometimes by her eloquent pleadings she was able to prevail with the officials; at other times they would be moved by nothing.

She early received permission to visit Mr. Judson in prison. And what sights and smells greeted her! The prison was just a rude shed that was never cleansed, vermin abounded, and the many prisoners sat or lay bound with chains or fast in the stocks. Mr. Judson wore three pairs of chains, and he carried scars from them till his dying day. A miserable place it was for this delicate, refined couple to meet; but how glad they were to find each other alive and to have the privilege of meeting even in such a place! Most of the time she had permission to carry him food. These privileges, however, cost her many presents and much money. She brought her husband some cushions also, and when he had the fever he surely would have died had she not obtained permission to build a bamboo booth within the prison and to give him some care.

After several months of this going and coming through the heat, or in times of greater danger, under cover of darkness, she could no longer visit him, for her little Maria was born. When her babe was two months old she received a note from her husband stating that he had been bound by five pairs of fetters and cast into the inner prison, his bamboo hovel torn down, and his cushions and mat taken from him. She went immediately to the governor who had usually befriended them, but he was not at home, and had left orders with his wife to tell Mrs. Judson should she call that she could not see him. But Mrs. Judson would not be so easily defeated. She came again at an hour when she knew he would be at home, and she so plead that he wept like a child. He promised he would not execute Mr. Judson, but said he could not release him from his present confinement and she must not ask it.

When the poor prisoner had been in the inner prison a month, he was taken again with fever. It was the hot season, and one hundred prisoners were shut in one room with no air except what could come through the cracks between the boards. She felt sure he must be removed from that place if he were to live. She first got permission to build a booth for herself near the prison (her home was two miles away), and she so incessantly begged the governor that he at last gave her permission to build a booth for her husband in another part of the prison, a miserable enough place, but a palace compared with the place he was then occupying. She also got permission to go in and out any time of the day to minister to him.

They were in this happy situation but a few days when she was summoned hastily by the governor. She was surprized when apparently for a trivial matter he had called her; but she soon learned that his real purpose was that she might not see her husband dragged away.

It was not without much difficulty she learned in which direction the prisoners had been taken. As soon as she knew, she made preparations to follow. With her she took little Maria, her two little Burman girls, and her Bengali cook. She made part of the trip by boat and part by a crude cart, and at Oung-pen-la, the end of her tiresome journey, found her husband in a more wretched place than before and in a more wretched condition, from having walked so many miles barefoot over the hot sand and gravel.

The only shelter she could get for herself was a grain-room of the guard-house, and there without any conveniences, not even a chair, she made her miserable abode for the next several months. It was a country place with no market, and she had a hard time buying supplies. Next morning after her arrival one of the Burman girls took smallpox. She was kept busy going back and forth carrying Maria, waiting on her husband and on the girl. Maria also took the smallpox. The children recovered, but the strenuous work and the many trying circumstances brought Mrs. Judson one of the diseases of the country usually fatal to foreigners. For two months she lay on the mat in their little room. During this time more than ever before was she thankful for her faithful Bengali servant. One of the most distressing things in connection with this illness was the cries of her little hungry Maria. She could not nurse the child, nor could she buy a drop of milk. By making presents to the jailers she got permission for Mr. Judson to carry the puny creature about the village begging a little milk from mothers who had young children.

What supported the suffering missionary through all these sore trials? She afterward wrote that she surely would have sunk beneath them had it not been for the consolations of religion. O Lord Jesus, help us to be more thankful for thy blessed consolations! They extend to every corner of the earth and to life's darkest hours. And help us to have more compassion for the millions who know nothing of thy consolations, who have no ray of light in their darkness!

Part III

SIX dreary months dragged by in Oung-pen-la, and then the glad news came that Mr. Judson was to be released from prison and sent to the Burmese camp as interpreter in negotiating with the English for peace. Mrs. Judson then returned to her house at Ava and felt more relieved than she had for many months. She was not there long until she was stricken with the spotted fever. As she was already so reduced in strength, she thought she should never survive. For a month she could not rise from her couch, and during this time came again sad news—that Mr. Judson had been returned from the camp and was to be sent back to Oung-pen-la. Then, if ever, did Mrs. Judson realize the value of prayer. To pray was all she could do. God comforted

HEROIC ANN JUDSON OF BURMA

her with a promise, and she felt sure her prayers would be answered.

And they were. The friendly governor secured Mr. Judson's release and took him to his own house, whither Mrs. Judson also was soon taken. They were kindly cared for there until they were allowed to pass out from under Burman rule. What a happy day it was when they reached the English camp!

But they loved the Burmans still and began a new mission among them at Amherst, in a part of the country under British control. The remnant of the church at Rangoon went with them, and good work was begun in the new field.

They had not settled long in Amherst when Mr. Judson had to leave for Ava as interpreter for the English. During his absence Mrs. Judson fell sick again with fever, and her broken constitution could hold up no longer. She was alone with the natives, the recruits from America having not yet arrived. In her last days she said little, but sometimes complained thus: "The teacher is long coming; and the new missionaries are long in coming; I must die alone and leave my little one; but as it is the will of God, I acquiesce in his will. I am not afraid of death, but I am afraid I shall not be able to bear these pains. Tell the teacher that the disease was most violent, and I could not write; tell him how I suffered and died; tell him all that you see; and take care of the house and the things till he returns." After she ceased noticing anything else, she would call her child to her and tell the nurse to be very kind to it until its father's return. On the twenty-fourth of October, 1826, when she was thirty-seven, her beautiful soul was released from its shattered prison and flew away to God.

Sadness steals over us when we think of the great sufferings this heroic soul endured. Yet we join with her husband when he says: "Oh, with what meekness and patience, and magnanimity, and Christian fortitude, she bore those sufferings! And can I wish they had been less? Can I sacriligiously wish to rob her crown of a single gem? Much she saw and suffered of the evil of this world, and eminently was she qualified to relish and enjoy the pure and holy rest into which she has entered." According to our glorious gospel, the sufferings of her earthly pilgrimage are not worthy to be compared with the glory that shall be revealed in her. A great harvest was reaped from the seed she helped to sow; and how shall she rejoice when she sees around the great white throne many who would not have attained that bliss had she not toiled and suffered in Burma!

A MODERN MIRACLE
Part I—Buddie: His Childhood Home

FAR back in the mountains of Tennessee, one hundred miles from a railroad and fifteen miles from a post-office, stood an old, weather-beaten log house. If you had visited that dwelling some fifty years ago, you might have seen a bareheaded, barefoot, ragged boy playing about its door with his little ragged sisters and their shaggy dog. This boy was Buddie.

Just inside the door, busily engaged at the spinning-wheel or the loom, you would have noticed a tall, slender woman. This was Buddie's mother. She had thirteen children to clothe, and she herself had to card the wool, spin it, and weave it into cloth before she could begin to sew their garments together with her needle and thread. Do you wonder that Buddie and his little sisters were ragged?

Buddie's father was a "moonshiner," so called in the mountainous districts of Tennessee. He carried on his business interests contrary to lawful methods. Although he had been careful to locate his distillery far back in the mountains, in a place not easily accessible to ordinary passers-by, still he lived in suspense lest the officers might discover a clue that would lead to his arrest. He trained his older boys to follow his occupation.

Each evening when the red-faced sun slipped away behind the mountain and dark shadows came stealing up from the east, a fear crept into the hearts of Buddie and his little sisters. No; it was not a fear of the darkness nor of the fancied goblins darkness contained, but a fear exceeding in terribleness the former kind. How will Father come home tonight? Will he come stumbling through the door, drink-crazed, as he has often done before? Will he seize one of us and beat that one unmercifully for some trivial offense? Will he abuse Mother? Such thoughts as these crowded into their minds, and filled them with terror when the first faint clatter of their father's steps sounded up the stony mountain path leading from the roadway below.

But I must tell you something more about the house Buddie lived in. It consisted of one room, with a dirt floor. It had one door and no windows. A home-made bed, built against one side of the room, was the only sleeping-place visible. A long, home-made table built at the opposite side of the room, a few boxes for chairs, a spinning-wheel, and a loom completed the furnishings. A big iron pot swung above the open fireplace at one end of the room, where Buddie's mother cooked their meals. You are wondering, no doubt, where Buddie and his brothers and sisters slept. When quiet at last settled over that dwelling it found all the children lying on a dirty quilt spread on the dirty floor, sleeping alongside their play fellow, the dog. Such was Buddie's childhood home.

Part II—Buddie's First Glimpse of Christianity

WHEN Buddie was about ten years old his father would send him to the mill, eight miles distant, to have corn ground for meal. One wintry day while Buddie was trudging along the winding road leading to the mill, he met a boy who lived on the other side of the mountain. Although this boy wore a cap, a nice warm coat, mittens, and shoes, he did not ridicule poor ragged little Buddie, but was kind to him. When they came to the parting of their ways, he invited Buddie to come over

A MODERN MIRACLE 49

Washington at the signing of the Declaration of Independence

to his home sometime and spend the night. Buddie agreed to do this if he could obtain his parents' consent.

Several days later found our little mountaineer sturdily pushing his way through the underbrush, climbing over rocks, crossing ravines, and following winding hog-trails through the woods, "goin' visitin'." This was to be a great event in his life—how great, he did not fully realize until years later. At last, after hours of weary trudging, he came into an opening where he saw a good-sized log house, several times larger than the one he called home. A volume of smoke was curling lazily above the great stone chimney. (A rude mud chimney built only part way up to the roof was the kind Buddie was accustomed to seeing in his neighborhood.) The dogs barked, and soon Buddie caught sight of his new friend coming out of a door and running down the path to meet him.

Buddie's friend led him into the house, where they met the other members of the family. After a little time for conversation, a call came from an adjoining room announcing supper. The man of the house led the way into the large dining-room, where Buddie saw for the first time in his life a table laden with appetizing foods. How hungry Buddie was! How much he wanted to seize a chunk of meat or bread and devour it at once! But he observed the orderly behavior of the other children, and he tried to do as they did. When they were all seated around the table, Buddie was surprized to see every one bow the head while the father repeated a few words. Buddie wondered to whom the man was talking and why they all acted so queerly. He had never before heard any one return thanks to God for food.

Then one by one the plates were passed and the father

A MODERN MIRACLE 51

heaped each one full of food and passed them back. Buddie could scarcely realize that he was entitled to such a liberal portion. He smelled the food and wished he might keep it just to smell of it. But a gnawing pain in his stomach urged him to eat, and soon he was greedily devouring the contents of his plate. Again and again his plate was refilled, until he could eat no more. His appetite had never before been completely satisfied, and this seemed too wonderful to be true.

After supper the children romped and played happily for several hours. Buddie noticed the father and mother sitting side by side before the fire, talking quietly together as if they loved each other. This looked strange to him, for he had never seen his parents act in such a manner. By and by the father called the children from their play and told them it was bedtime. Then he took a book down from the shelf, and all the children sat quietly listening while he read a chapter from the Bible. Buddie was more astonished than ever. He had never seen a book before, and now he wondered why the old man was talking to that object he held in his hands. What strange words he was saying to it! When the chapter was finished the old man closed the book and they knelt down to pray. Buddie knelt too, for he tried to do as they did. And how the old man prayed! He mentioned every one of his children and last of all he prayed for the poor little ignorant boy. "Make a man of him, O Lord," he prayed. "Make a useful man, one that will bless the world and bring a knowledge of thy saving grace to his fellow men." Buddie listened, and thought to himself, "Why, he didn't talk that way about *his* boys!"

After family prayer the children were put to bed. The old man led Buddie into a bedroom, removed some of his soiled clothing, tucked him into a featherbed, and covered him warmly with a woolly blanket. Buddie's wildest fancies had never pictured such luxuries and comfort as this!

Morning dawned all too quickly for Buddie, and after another sumptuous meal he started back to the wretched hovel whence he had come. Twelve weary miles stretched before him, but as he retraced his steps of yesterday he recalled the happy hours he had just spent and the wonderful things he had heard and seen, and a glad, new joy filled his childish soul.

Part III—Buddie's Father's Death; Life on the Texas Frontier

SOME years before Buddie reached manhood, death entered his home, seized his father, and carried him into the great unknown world. That was a sad time. As the bleary-faced, wretched man lay dying, the officers entered his home to place him under arrest. They had found him at last, but too late.

How the poor widowed mother managed to keep her half-starved children alive is hard to tell. Several years later she removed with the youngest members of the family to Texas, where they tasted of frontier life. Buddie secured a position as cowboy on a large ranch. Here he learned to mount high-spirited horses, dash away across the plains, rope wild steers, and perform the various feats of a Western cattleman. He also learned to play cards, gamble, and participate in the deepest and darkest of sins known in frontier life.

One evening after the boys had returned to their shanty for supper, they observed a lone man on horseback approaching. He rode up to the door, dismounted,

A MODERN MIRACLE 53

and exchanged greetings with the boys, then informed them that he had come to spend the night at their lodging. They invited him indoors, glad to share their simple store with a stranger; for life on a ranch is so very monotonous that hospitality thrives there. Supper being ready, they sat down to eat. As usual, the boys prepared to rush hurriedly at the food, when the stranger interrupted them, saying, "Wait a minute, boys!" Then he bowed his head, and returned thanks to God for the food. Buddie's heart smote him. He had heard something like that once before! How vividly he recalled his visit to that Christian home during his childhood!

The boys had planned to spend the evening at playing cards, but the minister had planned otherwise. And the minister carried out his plans. After supper had ended, he drew from his saddle-bags a book, sat down, and began to read aloud to the boys. Buddie felt sure that the book was the same kind the old Christian gentleman had read from at family prayer. After reading a while, the minister knelt and prayed. He voiced his supplication in very strong language, telling the Lord how wicked those boys were, and mentioning details of their meanness as accurately as though he had been personally acquainted with them. He prayed for them earnestly, touchingly, until Buddie trembled with conviction. Louder and louder rose his voice, until Buddie thought the wrath of Almighty God was ready to fall upon them. "If he doesn't quit soon," reasoned poor Buddie, "I'll be a dead man." When at last his prayer was ended, not one of the boys felt inclined to begin a game of cards. And so they passed the evening listening to the minister's words.

Immediately after breakfast the next morning the boys prepared to go out as usual, when the minister again drew out his Bible and asked them to remain a while for reading and prayer. Once more Buddie felt an awful, invisible power seize him and throw him into a state of misery. He felt that he could not endure life much longer in such a state. After prayer they brought the minister's horse to the door, where he mounted and prepared to leave them. "I'll be back in a month, boys," he assured them, not waiting for an invitation to return, and then he rode away.

Part IV—The Revival Meeting; Buddie's Conversion

MUCH speculation followed the minister's visit at the ranch-house. "He's just an old hypocrite, and he'll never come back," said one of the boys. "He isn't!" insisted Buddie. "And you'll see he will be back again as good as his word." Secretly, Buddie dreaded his return, yet he believed heartily that the minister would visit them again.

When the month had passed by, one evening the boys observed their former visitor approaching their shack as he had come before. They hurried out to meet him, each one eager to be first to clasp his hand in greeting. He dismounted again, and gave his horse into Buddie's charge. Somehow—Buddie could not understand why —he felt afraid of that horse. Although he had ridden the roughest, wildest horses on the ranch, he did not have the courage to mount this old gray mare and ride her to the corral. So he took her by the bridle and led her away.

The minister's second visit produced much the same effect upon the boys as his first had produced. Buddie's misery was intensified until he thought he could bear no more.

A MODERN MIRACLE 55

Through the labors of this traveling minister, a large, old-fashioned revival arbor-meeting was arranged for. People came many miles across the plains in their "prairie-schooners" to attend this meeting, and the camp was thickly populated. Buddie and his mother were there. Buddie had never before heard such preaching nor such shouting. The praying reminded him forcibly of the traveling minister's prayers at the ranch-house, and invariably affected him in the same disagreeable manner. Conviction for him at last grew intolerable, and Buddie feared what the end might be. Although this minister was not bald-headed, nor clad in a long-tailed coat like the traveling minister had been, still he seemed to know just as much about Buddie's meanness and, to Buddie's discomfort, pictured him publicly when describing the wretched state of a man in sin.

One night when the invitation was given, Buddie resolved to go forward for prayer. Then the tempter reminded him of his uncouth appearance, and of the dangerous weapon that protruded suspiciously from his left hip-pocket. "They'll arrest you for carrying arms," the tempter said. But Buddie was too miserable to argue any longer with fears, so he pressed his way forward. Here he found peace with God.

The transformation wrought in his soul was too wonderful to find expression in words. Buddie lay awake all night, gazing up into the starry heavens and praising the Lord for amazing grace which "saves to the uttermost."

Soon afterward Buddie attended Sunday-school for the first time in his life, and there he was given a copy of the New Testament. Although he could not read, he began at once to study the letters, and before long was able to spell. Then he began at the first chapter of his Testament, and, spelling each word separately, he laboriously applied himself to the reading of God's Word.

Many years have passed since Buddie's glorious conversion, still he rejoices to tell of the wonderful love of God, which reached down from the heights of bliss to the depths of wretchedness, picked him up, cleaned him inside and outside, made a man of him, then sent him out into the world to preach the everlasting gospel of the Son of God.

DOROTHEA LYNDE DIX

EVERY stitch even and in its right place or it must be ripped out. This was the way Dorothea Lynde Dix learned to sew; for Grandmother Dix believed in the strictest order and neatness, and not only in sewing, but in all her work. And it was well for Dorothea that she had such a grandmother, for from her she inherited many of the sterling qualities that characterized her later life.

On the other hand, Dorothea's parents, especially her father, led a shiftless, aimless life, wandering from place to place, seeking to better the family financially, but never accomplishing their aim. Thus, at home Dorothea had practically no opportunities; her schooling was interrupted, and she received no systematic domestic or intellectual training.

At the age of twelve her eager, enterprising spirit could no longer bear to be held down by the poverty which this aimless life brought on. So without stopping to say good-by to her parents, she left home and went to live with her grandparents in Boston.

There Dorothea had good opportunities for attending school, and made rapid progress in her studies. At the age of fourteen she opened a school for children in Worcester. She was so young that she put on long skirts to appear older. But she inherited her grandmother's dignity and strict discipline, and demanded obedience to the rules of the school. Her pupils respected her authority and obeyed her.

Dorothea determined to become still more efficient, so she returned to the home of her grandparents to qualify herself to instruct older pupils. After a while she took

58 BITS OF BIOGRAPHY

Washington's tomb

a class of day-pupils in a small house belonging to her grandmother. At the age of nineteen she opened a boarding- and day-school in the Dix mansion. She had her ideal of what a school should be and spared neither time nor strength to make it such. Through her thorough and careful methods she had gained popularity as a teacher and received into her school scholars from some of the most prominent families in Boston and other Northeastern towns.

At this time Grandfather Dix was dead and Mrs. Dix was in poor health, so that Dorothea had charge of the family affairs as well as of the school. Several pupils, including her two young brothers, boarded with her. She was housekeeper, mother, teacher, and superintendent, as well as nurse for her grandmother. She enjoyed these responsibilities, but they, together with her ambition to make her school an ideal one, were a tax on her strength. Still she was not satisfied. Her heart went out to the poor, unfortunate children about her, and she felt that she must do something for them. But first she must give attention to her brothers and other pupils and fit them for their life-work. Finally she conceived a plan to start a school for poor children over the stable of the Dix mansion. Her grandmother, who was not given much to charitable deeds, at first opposed her, but afterward gave her consent.

The barn-school was a grand success, but with her many other responsibilities was so detrimental to Dorothea's health that she was obliged to take a rest. At the invitation of Dr. William Channing she became tutor of his children for six months, spending most of that period at their summer home on Narragansett Bay, R. I. Later she went with that family to the West Indies.

Returning home in much better health, she resumed

her school responsibilities with renewed activity and improved methods. Her school grew so rapidly that she was unable to receive all the applicants. A prominent feature of the school was the formation of moral and religious character. She felt that her mission was so to train her pupils that they would be able to be a blessing in the world, and she was determined to accomplish this at any cost. Overwork brought on another failure in health, and she took a trip to England, where under the best care that kind friends could give her she regained her health.

After her return to America, Miss Dix became particularly interested in the care of the insane. She visited asylums and jails where they were confined and aroused the public sentiment by her reports of their pitiable condition and heartless treatment. In each State where she made investigation she brought the matter before the State Legislature, and though often bitterly opposed, in every case she obtained legislation and funds to better the conditions of these unfortunate people. In Providence, R. I., she secured fifty thousand dollars for an asylum from a multi-millionaire who had never before been known to give to charitable purposes.

In her trips through the country she often encountered great dangers. Once in Michigan she hired a carriage to go through an uninhabited part of the country. The young driver carried two pistols for protection from robbers. Fearing the lad would use the weapons unwisely, Miss Dix had him give them to her. Sure enough, they were attacked by a robber, but she calmly said, "Are you not ashamed to rob a woman? What little money I have, I need to defray my expenses in visiting prisons and poorhouses. But if you are in need of money, I will give you some." This speech stunned the

DOROTHEA LYNDE DIX

robber, for he recognized her voice, having heard her lecture in a Philadelphia prison. He apologized for his outrage and allowed her to continue her journey.

Miss Dix was invited to Canada, Nova Scotia, Newfoundland, and to Great Britain, where she continued her great mission. She also explored the realms of misery, sorrow, and woe throughout Europe. There she spent two years, making thorough investigations.

Shortly before the Civil War, Miss Dix returned to the United States, and when the crisis came, she offered her services as nurse. She was appointed superintendent of women nurses. After serving her country loyally throughout the years of the war, she refused recognition offered her by way of public meetings and large sums of money, but accepted instead two beautiful flags from the Government.

The last five years of her life Miss Dix spent in retirement in a hospital at Trenton, N. J., which she had established. She died in 1887, at the age of eighty-three years.

MARGARET FULLER OSSOLI

MARGARET was especially fond of her mother, and she had good reasons to be, for Mrs. Fuller was a sweet-tempered woman, whose religion pervaded her whole life and made it beautiful.

Margaret's father was a distinguished lawyer and a member of the Massachusetts State Legislature several times and a member of Congress from 1817 to 1825. He was a friend of John Quincy Adams.

Her paternal grandfather was a graduate of Harvard University and a Congregational minister. Though he was patriotic, he voted against the Constitution of the United States in the State convention called to accept it. His reason was that it recognized slavery. This anti-slavery principle which was demonstrated in her grandfather, as well as other relatives, had considerable effect upon Margaret's life.

Margaret was a brilliant student, and her father took charge of her education. His ideas were fifty years in advance of those of his neighbors in regard to the education of girls. He had little confidence in the schools of his time, and so he became the sole instructor of his daughter. Margaret, being very ambitious, made rapid progress, to the great satisfaction of her father, but still he urged her on. At the age of six she commenced the study of Latin, and from time to time took up other studies according to her father's ideas. She was kept busy every hour of the day at various tasks. She could recite to no one but her father, and his business often delayed her recitations till late in the evening. He was a severe teacher. Thus her lessons were a heavy strain, and when she went to bed several hours too late, she was a victim of nightmares and horrible dreams. She was sometimes caught walking all about the house in her sleep.

After some time Margaret's lessons became less of a burden to her, and she pursued her study of the Latin writers with such a passion that she lost her appetite for food. Her health soon became so impaired that she was forced to have a change. She was sent to the school of the Misses Prescott at Groton, Mass. Here she won friends at first, but her oddities soon turned them against her. One time, upon being rebuked, through a trick of her schoolmates, for improper conduct, she fell into a nervous passion and knocked herself unconscious. Conditions grew worse until, when her nervous passions were again aroused over some trouble in the school, she knocked herself unconscious a second time. Her schoolmates, being alarmed, tried to arouse her and begged her forgiveness, but she did not respond. But in the several days that she lay in bed under the care of one of her teachers as nurse, she saw the sinful condition of her heart and almost despaired. Finally the teacher won her by love and by relating to her the touching story of her own sad life. This brought about a great change in Margaret; she took a new hold upon life, and hope sprang up within her. She called her schoolmates to her bedside and begged them to forgive her. They gladly and tenderly did so.

From then on Margaret devoted herself to self-culture, eager to become a blessing to mankind. She remained two years at the school and returned home at the age of fifteen, a remarkable and womanly girl. She placed herself under discipline. She rose before five in summer, walked one hour, practised on the piano one hour, had breakfast at seven, read French literature till eight, studied philosophy till nine-thirty, attended Greek school at twelve, practised on the piano till dinner, after an early dinner read Italian two hours, then walked or rode, and in the evening played and sang till eleven. Besides all this, she assisted with the household duties. She was willing to surmount any difficulties to bring her to her best. She pursued the study of foreign literature with great delight.

When she was twenty years old, Margaret began the instruction of the younger children of the family, while she still continued her studies and housework. In this manner she spent three years of the best part of her life. Though it impaired her health, she did not regret it, but only wanted the children to repay her by reaching the highest attainments in life.

At twenty-three she became teacher in Mr. Alcott's famous school in Boston, and later principal of Green Street Academy, Providence, R. I. She became a successful teacher, striving to develop in her pupils general activity of mind, accuracy in processes, and constant looking for principles and for the good and beautiful.

Dissatisfied with her sphere of usefulness and eager to pursue the higher branches of science, art, and literature, she resigned her position and removed to Jamaica Plain, near Boston. Here she divided her time between study and teaching private scholars foreign languages. She could teach seven languages: English, Latin, Greek, German, French, Italian, and Spanish.

Conversation was said to be her natural element, and conversation of an hour or two with her is said not only to have entertained and informed one, but to have made an epoch in one's life. She was persuaded to open a school of conversation in Boston, which was attended

MARGARET FULLER OSSOLI

by from twenty-five to forty ladies. The conversation was devoted to a variety of instructive subjects.

Some time after this Miss Fuller filled an important place on the editorial staff of Horace Greeley, the great antislavery editor. Besides her editorial work, she wrote a number of books and also translated the works of foreign writers.

For some time Margaret's Christian experience was clouded and unsettled, but through the influence of an older lady she received definite light in her soul and shortly after received the experience of sanctification.

In 1847, at the age of thirty-seven, she went to Europe and made her home in Rome. There she was married to Giovanni Angelo Marquis Ossoli, a citizen of rank. He became a patriotic follower of Mazzin, who led a movement for the independence of Italy. Mrs. Ossoli became nurse in the hospitals in the same cause. In 1849, when Rome was in a state of siege, she continued her work in hospitals, though the weather was intensely hot, her health delicate, and the dead and dying were lying all about her. Both she and her husband heroically faced grave dangers, but they survived the storm and went to Rieti, where they remained for several months. Leaving there, they went to Florence to take ship for America.

Before sailing, Mrs. Ossoli had strange forebodings, but they ventured the trip. Her dread was not unfounded. The first serious thing that happened was that the captain of the ship died of smallpox. Mrs. Ossoli's child took it, but recovered. Then, before they reached their destiny, the ship was wrecked in a terrific gale. When hope was past, Mrs. Ossoli placed her child in the hands of the steward for safety, and then she and her husband went down together. The steward was washed ashore with the dead child in his arms, and the baby was buried in the sand. Mrs. Ossoli's trunk, containing her correspondence with her husband and other important papers, was washed ashore. These were valuable to her friends, as they contained some important history of her life.

SOME OF AUNT HARRIET'S EXPERIENCES

"NO, HONEY, I don't have much longer for this world. I go round now bent over with my nose nearly touching my big toe, but I have not forgot what the Lord has done for me."

"Aunt Harriet, the Lord has done much for all of us, but you have lived a long life, you could tell us many things."

"This is my ninety-first birthday, child, and I have had experiences that would make you wonder."

Every twelve-year-old who reads this should stop right here and thank God for the blessings he enjoys. When Aunt Harriet was just twelve years old she was taken from her mother and playmates and all former associates. She was stood on a block and sold at auction to the highest bidder, just as pigs and colts and calves are often sold. She was then sent to new and strange quarters and set to work with the slaves —to hoe and plow and build up the plantation that belonged to her master.

She went out with men day after day and month after month and year after year to split rails, cut ditches, throw up levees—and all this as she was growing into womanhood. She did as a dumb animal would do, for if she answered back or failed to appear, she suffered the consequences. The overseer was always ready with his lash to cut to the blood of every slave who failed to do the master's will. So Aunt Harriet only laughed and donned men's overalls and asked them to call her "Bill."

As she grew older she was pressed into domestic

service. There she learned to cook. And if she did not manage to suit the tastes of her exacting family, the lash came down again.

Frequently under such treatment the slaves would endeavor to hide or run away, but ignorant of the ways of the world and of their own abilities, their efforts brought no satisfaction.

Once Aunt Harriet joined a party who were stealing away at night. Each took a blanket and rolled himself up as small as possible and undertook to hide in a ditch. Aunt Harriet, however, observing that the ditch had no top covering, decided to slip into a hole or wallow of some kind under a culvert. Thus, when the others were discovered and driven back, she escaped alone into the woods. Without any knowledge of the geography of her country or its resources, she remained in the woods for months living often on the herbs and grasses that she found, which she ate without seasoning. She chose to do this rather than to return to her master.

One day she was joined by another slave-woman, who had escaped, and together they decided to leave the woods and find other quarters. To do this it was necessary to cross a shallow lake, or swamp.

As they stepped into the shiny waters, Aunt Harriet felt a sensation as of something giving way under her feet; but she skipped across quickly from one hard substance to another. Before her feet touched the farther shore, she heard a splashing and a crunching, and on looking back, to her horror, she saw her companion was being gulped down by what she at the time supposed to be "big fish" but afterwards learned were alligators.

Screaming with terror and calling for help, she was soon discovered and taken again into bondage by her former cruel master. She was soundly beaten and also

AUNT HARRIET'S EXPERIENCES 69

compelled to drink a pint of castor-oil, which perhaps was for the purpose of renovating her system from what-

Aunt Harriet

ever disorders it may have received from her woods diet.

In course of time Aunt Harriet was married.

"No, child, you could not have told my man from a

white man—white skin, blue eyes, and tall and straight as a hickory limb."

"And you were good looking too, Aunt Harriet, when you were young?"

"Yes, yes; that is a fact. I was straight too, and round and plump."

About the time of her marriage there was much agitation concerning the slave-trade. The North was in sympathy with the slave. Some ways of escape were now opening; after this couple had been married but a short time, the husband decided to find a home for his bride. He ran away to Vicksburg. For a time, his nationality or race color being undiscovered, he obtained work in a printing-office. However, he never felt safe.

Later, Aunt Harriet, alone and much abused, left the plantation and found work and protection in a river town. But one day when she heard a boat whistle she decided to make safety more likely by finding work on a boat that would land her in some more distant land. She hurried to meet the coming boat and requested work. She was well received. The next day she met the captain and was given her orders. A great surprize was now in store, for the tall man cook on the boat came joyfully forward exclaiming to the captain and other by-standers, "This is my wife, this is my wife."

A joyful reunion was held and for forty years this man and wife journeyed together, until the husband was called away by the death angel. His last exhortations were for his dear wife to mend her ways and to meet him in heaven, where parting never comes.

Aunt Harriet has now gone to heaven, too.

A GREAT REFORMER

MORE than four hundred years ago in the little village of Eisleben, Saxony, was born a baby boy who was destined to some day arouse the world. His parents

Martin Luther

were very poor, though pious, God-fearing people. They desired much to bring the little fellow up for God. When he was one day old, he was christened in the

Roman Catholic Church, and named Martin in honor of one of the early saints. The father would often kneel by the bedside of his little son, invoke God's richest blessings upon him, and pray that God would give the little fellow grace to remember that his name, Luther, meant purity, and that he must sometime advance the cause of true religion.

At a very early age he was sent to school. He was not taught what children in America are taught today. He had to spend much of his time in the church-edifice, learning prayers, praying to the Virgin and the saints, studying Latin; and learning church music. His father often invited learned men to their home, thinking Martin would be greatly benefited by their conversations.

He remained in school until eighteen years of age. During this time, he studied hard and soon surpassed all his classmates. He had a cheerful, joyous disposition, which caused him to be loved and admired by both teachers and pupils. One day on being asked as to the secret of his success, he replied, "To pray well is the better half of study." He never began a day's work without first praying to God to help him that day.

When he was eighteen his father was able to send him to a university. One day about two years after he had gone to the university, he, while looking over some books in the library, spied a very large old-looking book he had never seen before. It was fastened with heavy clasps. On opening it, he found the words "Biblia Sacra," meaning Holy Bible.

Eagerly he turned over the leaves, stopping now and then to read. Soon he came to the story of Hannah and little Samuel. "What a treasure!" he thought. How he longed to have such a book that he might read it through! So day after day when he could spare time

A GREAT REFORMER

from his studies, he would go into the library and read and study this Bible. As he read and studied, he came to see himself a sinner. He longed to become holy and live a consecrated life for God. Though he had been taught to pray, yet he had never realized the experience of having his sins forgiven.

Many times Martin would fast and pray that God might save him. One day as he was going to prayers, the Lord revealed to him how he might be forgiven and made free. He then started out on his great reform against the Roman Catholic Church. This meant much, but he counted not his life dear unto himself. Many times his life was in danger. At one time his friends concealed him in a prison.

When he went out, he dressed as a knight so that no one would know him. One day he saw some people whom he knew, but he dared not let them know who he was. Though much of his time was spent behind bolts and bars, yet he was not idle. He wrote volume after volume, and translated part of the Scriptures.

From this on until the end of his life, he declared Christ, who had set him free. His last labors were those of love and peace, and though he has been dead many years, his life and influence still live, and they can never be forgotten.

IMPRISONED FOR THE GLORY OF GOD

LUTHER'S persecutors became so angered because of his bold actions at the Diet of Worms that they determined to dispose of him speedily. While Luther, in company with his brother and a Mr. Amsdorff, was passing through a forest on his way home from that great council, he was seized by five masked men. His brother escaped, Mr. Amsdorff and the driver were held at some distance from the carriage, but Luther was quickly covered with a military cloak and placed upon a horse. This done, the men leaped upon their horses and with Luther as their captive galloped away into the forest. They soon retraced their steps by another path, however, and continued making many windings in order to utterly baffle any attempt to track them.

About one hour before midnight they reached the foot of a mountain on the summit of which was an old castle surrounded on all sides by the black forests of Thuringia. It was to this old fortress that Luther was conducted. He was led through the iron gates, which were closed and barred behind him. He dismounted in the court, and one of his captors took him to the room that was to be his prison. His ministerial garb was taken from him, and garments of military style given him instead. He was commanded to let his beard and hair grow, so that no one in the castle might discover who he was. Thus the great reformer was imprisoned by his friends in order to protect him from his enemies.

God had wonderfully planned; Luther was now far from his enemies and danger, secure from turmoil and confusion. In this secluded spot he gave himself to prayer, meditation, and rest. He wrote to one: "Your prayers are the only thing I need. At last I am at rest."

His calmness, however, was not of long duration. He thought of the needs of his people, and his very soul longed to be out in the fight. He thought he was spending his time in shameful indolence. "I am here all day," wrote he, "in idleness and pleasures. I am reading the Bible in Hebrew and Greek. I am going to write a treatise in German. I shall continue the translation of the Psalms, and compose a volume of sermons as soon as I receive what I want from Wittenberg." And yet he says, "Woe is me; I live in idleness, in sleep, and indolence."

Luther's enemies thought that if he were not dead at least they should hear no more of him. But their joy was soon to be disturbed, for behold a multitude of writings, composed in the Wartburg, rapidly succeeded each other, and the beloved words of Luther were everywhere received with gladness. He was fighting against error and defending God's cause as really as if he were still in the midst of the battle, though it did not seem so to him. His friends at Wittenberg soon found out where he was, and great was their rejoicing when they knew he was alive and safe from harm. They informed him from time to time as to the conditions of the church. Having no strong leader, false teachers crept in among them and some of God's own flock were influenced by the false doctrines. When Luther learned of the danger, he could scarcely refrain from breaking away from his prison to go to them.

Finally the trouble became so widespread and the confusion so great that he could stand it no longer. He decided to go to their rescue at any cost. He knew it might mean his death, but he trusted God and set forth. His military guise kept him from being recognized, and God brought him in safety to Wittenberg. His presence was hailed with great joy by his faithful friends, and he was soon proclaiming the truth as boldly as he did before his imprisonment. Peace and harmony were soon restored among the believers; the fanatical prophets quit the field; and Luther, by God's help, accomplished the work for which he had left his retreat.

Now he was free to turn his attention again to the Scriptures, which he had been translating into the German language. The printing of the New Testament was carried on with untiring zeal, and on Sept. 21, 1522, three thousand copies in the German language were ready for the people. The Scriptures, written for the first time in the language of the German people, charmed and moved all classes. So eager were the people for the Word of Truth that they seized the pages spread before them as a letter coming from heaven. It was their own Book, the very Book of God, and did more than all Luther's preaching and writings toward the spread of real Christian living. Each one could now hear the voice of God for himself.

During those months when Luther was behind the dark walls of Wartburg Castle, when he thought his life was almost in vain, when he could not see nor feel that any good whatever was being accomplished by him, at that very time God was using him as an instrument to bring about the salvation of more souls and more glory to God than in all the years of his active labors.

As Christians in a spiritual warfare, we may have to pass through a Wartburg Castle, but let us not be fearful or discouraged. It may be a part of God's plan for us, and our attitude while there may be the means of bringing more glory to God than those times when we feel we are on the mountain-top of usefulness.

THE WESLEYS AND THEIR WORK

OF MANY persons who have become great it can be said that the foundation for the character that gave them such note was laid early in life by the counsel of a wise father or the instruction of a good mother. With the Wesleys it was a combination of the two.

The father was a clergyman and a real example of what a man in that calling should be. He possessed a firm and manly character, practical sense, and habits active and unwearied. The mother was a remarkable woman. She possessed a sanctified wisdom, a masculine understanding, and in her disposition was calm and reflecting. She knew Latin and Greek and was the instructress of her children. It seems she was particularly interested in her son John, who, when about six years old, had a providential and singular escape from being burned to death, when the parsonage was being consumed.

Mrs. Wesley considered herself under special obligation to be "more careful of the soul of a child whom God had thus so mercifully provided for." Under such care the little John became serious very early in life, and at the age of eight years was given permission to partake of the sacrament. At the age of eleven he was sent to school at the Charter House, where he was noted for his diligence and progress in learning. So quiet and regular was he in his manners and habits that he became the favorite of his master. At the age of seventeen he began school at Oxford, where he pursued his studies with great advantage. For a time his desire was to make a show in languages and philosophy and he laxed into a sort of religious carelessness that he might succeed in his ambition, but he became awakened and later wrote,

John Wesley

"But that desire is past. There is a more excellent way."

His mother in answering said, "I hope that God's Holy Spirit by taking off your relish for earthly enjoyment may prepare and dispose your mind for a more serious and close application to things of a more

THE WESLEYS AND THEIR WORK 79

sublime and spiritual nature. In good earnest, resolve to make religion the business of your life, for after all that is the one thing which, strictly speaking, is necessary. All things beside are comparatively little to the purposes of life. To know whether or not you have salvation is a matter that deserves great consideration." And such excellent advice was not lost upon the youthful John, for his intimate correspondence with his parents was the principal means under God of producing a still more decided change in the young man a little later.

The summer of 1726 he spent at home conversing freely with his parents upon those serious topics, which fully occupied his mind. In September he returned to Oxford, where he was acknowledged as a man of talents and an excellent critic in the learned languages. In November he was chosen as Greek lecturer and moderator in the classes, but about two years later he began to give more attention to religious duties.

He had a faithful companion and coworker in his brother Charles, and while at their school they were "faithful in that which is little." They, with two other young men, joined later by others, formed a little society and began spending some evenings each week in reading and studying the Bible. Later they took up another work, and a letter written by a friend tells of what it consisted.

"Their undertaking included these several particulars—to converse with young students; to visit prisons; to instruct some poor families; to take care of a school. They took great pains with the younger members of the university to rescue them from bad company and to encourage them in a sober, studious life.

"Some one or other of them went to the jail every

day. They read in the chapel to as many prisoners as would attend, and when a new prisoner came their conversation was close and searching."

But for this way of serving God they received great opposition, and the sarcasm and ridicule became too strong for one of their number, and he deserted. John sought his father's counsel by letter, and how the two brothers must have taken courage on receiving the reply. For the father blessed God who had given his two sons grace and courage to turn war against the world and the devil. He bade them defy reproach and to go on in the path to which the Savior had directed them.

"This day," said he, "I received both yours, and this evening in the course of our reading I found an answer that I thought would be more proper than any I myself could dictate. 'Great is my glorying of you. I am filled with comfort. I am exceeding joyful.' For my part, on the present view of your actions, my daily prayers are that God will keep you humble. I am sure if you continue to suffer for righteousness' sake the Spirit of God and of glory will in some good measure rest upon you. Be never weary of well doing; never look back, for you know the crown and prize are before you. Be not high-minded, but fear. Preserve an equal temper of mind under whatever treatment you meet with. Bear no more sail than is necessary, but steer steady. He by whom actions and intentions are weighed will accept, esteem, and reward you." And their brother Samuel wrote, "Stand thou stedfast as a beaten anvil. For it is the part of a good champion to be flayed alive and to conquer."

Thus encouraged the brothers redoubled their efforts. Of John it is said that he thought prayer to be more his business than anything else. And he often came out of

THE WESLEYS AND THEIR WORK

his closet with a "serenity of countenance next to shining."

In 1732 John extended his work out into country districts, making the journeys mostly on foot. His difficulties were many, but he was still unshaken. And toward the end of the year his friends became alarmed at his poor state of health. About this time too he lost the wise counsels of his father through his father's death, and not feeling led to take up his father's work, as friends desired him to do, he, with his brother, made ready to sail to America with Mr. Oglethorpe.

"Our end, in leaving our own country," said they, "is not to avoid want (God having given us plenty of temporal blessings), nor to gain the dung or dross of riches or honor; but singly this: to 'save' our souls; to live wholly to the glory of God."

But it seems the time for getting the gospel to the Indians was not yet ripe, for on the first visit of the Wesleys to these heathen the spokesman replied, "Our enemies are all about us, and we can do nothing but fight; but if the beloved ones should ever give us to be at peace, then we would hear the great word." So, after about two years of great sacrifice in the new land, with little results, the Wesleys were found again in England where some time later they began a laborious but glorious ministry which resulted in the salvation of many souls.

They had large views of usefulness, for they considered the world their parish. Wherever they were invited, they preached the doctrine of salvation by faith. "Many," said Mr. John Wesley, "only wait till we have leisure to instruct them. Till our gracious Master sends more laborers into the harvest, my time is much too little."

In London great crowds followed him. He labored in churches, rooms, houses, and prisons; and the results of these efforts were powerful and lasting. When churches were closed against him, he, often to thousands of people, preached in the open air, by which means, he said, Providence had made a way for myriads, who never troubled any church, to find the way of salvation. His conduct; his spirit, gentle, tender, and sympathizing; his courage, bold and undaunted; his patience; his charity; his wonderful activity; and his endurance—all caused men to wonder. In fact, he and his brother Charles were recognized as men separated to the gospel of God. Their preaching greatly affected the people. Some trembled, others wailed. Some, while prayers were being offered for them, rose up with a sudden change of feeling, testifying that they were saved.

To follow these devout men into more extended fields of labor means that we shall follow them into formidable contests and into persecutions abundant. They were attacked by the press, frowned upon by church authorities, insulted by violent mobs, and arraigned before civil magistrates. But they learned not to be discouraged if the fruits of their efforts did not always appear immediately. With calm heroism they prosecuted their labors, and shrank from no dangers, but firmly trusted their lives into the hands of God. And from John Wesley's journal we obtain glimpses of him at a ripe old age braving storms and tempests, fearless of the winter snow or summer heat.

On his eighty-fifth birthday Mr. Wesley had these reflections: "I this day enter on my eighty-fifth year. And what cause have I to praise God, as for a thousand spiritual blessings, so for bodily blessings also! How little have I suffered yet, by the 'rush of numerous years'! It is true, I am not so agile as I was in times past: I do not run or walk so fast as I did. My sight is a little decayed. My left eye is grown dim, and hardly serves me to read. I have daily some pain in my right eye. I find likewise some decay in my memory. I find no decay in my hearing, smell, taste, or appetite, nor do I feel any such thing as weariness either in traveling or preaching. To what cause can I impute this, that I am as I am? First, doubtless to the power of God, fitting me for the work to which I am called, as long as he pleases to continue me therein; next, to the prayers of his children; to my constant exercise and change of air; to my never having lost a night's sleep, sick or well, at land or sea, since I was born; to my having constantly, for above sixty years, risen at four in the morning. Whether or not I am to quit shortly this tabernacle, I do not know: but be it one way or the other, I have only to say:

>"My remnant of days
>I spend to his praise
>Who died the whole world to redeem:
>Be they many or few,
>My days are his due,
>And they are all devoted to him."

Mr. Charles Wesley had a weak body and was in a poor state of health during the greater part of his life, which was probably due to his too close application to study, and his abstinence from food. His much horseback-riding probably contributed to lengthen out his life to a good old age. On Mar. 29, 1788, at the age of seventy-nine years, he died, and on April 5 was buried in Marybone Churchyard. On his tombstone are the following lines:

> "With poverty of spirit bless'd,
> Rest, happy saint, in Jesus rest;
> A sinner saved, through grace forgiven,
> Redeemed from earth to reign in heaven!
> Thy labors of unwearied love,
> By thee forgot, are crowned above;
> Crowned through the mercy of thy Lord,
> With a free, full, immense reward!"

Beginning with the year 1790, Mr. John Wesley realized that his end was now approaching. "I find I grow old," he says, "and should I take thought for the morrow, I would be weighed down by the increase of bodily infirmities." Notwithstanding this, he still acted under the impression, "I must be about my Father's business."

On Feb. 21, 1791, he preached what proved to be his last sermon. His last days were beautiful, and his death was an admirable close to so laborious and useful a life. He often called together his attendants and asked them to pray. At those times his whole soul seemed to revel in the blessings of God. Among his last words were, "The clouds drop fatness, but the best of all is, God is with us."

One who was with him much during his last days said: "So fine an old man I never saw. The happiness of his mind beamed forth in his countenance. Every look showed how fully he enjoyed the remembrance of a life well spent. In him even old age appeared delightful, like an evening without a cloud. It was impossible to observe him without wishing fervently, 'May my latter end be like his.'"

LINCOLN AND HIS MOTHER

"HOW American history would dwindle," says Mr. Gallaher, "if the name of Abraham Lincoln were taken out of it! Grant was great; Lee was great; many others have been and are great in all the walks of life

Abraham Lincoln

But Lincoln, who came out of the lowly heart of the people, will come back nearer to that heart than any other man probably that the nation has known. There have been men of war, and there have been men of peace; but there has been no such man of peace in war as Lincoln.

"Why is it we never tire of thinking of Mr. Lincoln personally, nor of speaking of him and his deeds? Is it not because 'he was indeed one of the most unique figures in history, and one of the most remarkable surprizes of the age'? What has he been called by those who knew him best? 'The greatest of patriots, the wisest of rulers, the ablest of men.'"

What led to his greatness? Says one, "His readiness to grasp the right and his decision to go forward in the pathway of duty." "He was richly blessed with a spirit of forgiveness, bearing malice toward none," says another. And from the lips of a number of others come words like these: "He was simple and tender. He had the sterner qualities of a perfect man. He sought to say the thing that would stand the test of time and square itself with eternal justice. In him, as a thread of gold, running through all the inner experiences of his life was an unwavering faith in a divine Providence." But Lincoln attributed his greatness to a force not of himself. A short time before his death he said, "All that I am, and all that I hope to be, I owe to my mother."

That mother died when "Abe" was only nine years of age. But even then she had already woven the threads of her deepest character into the habits and purposes of her boy. Her own lot had been a humble one. Her father and mother had died when she was but nine years old, and Nancy Hanks (for that was her name) was left an orphan. She then found a home with an aunt, and there grew up a sweet-tempered, beautiful woman, famous at spinning and apt at housekeeping.

Finally she became acquainted with Thomas Lincoln, a carpenter, and on June 12, 1806, was married to him at the home of Richard Beery, near Beechland, Ky. The occasion was celebrated in the boisterous style of one

LINCOLN AND HIS MOTHER 87

hundred years ago. Mr. Graham, an eye-witness, says:
"I saw Nancy Hanks Lincoln at her wedding, a fresh-

Monument to the memory of Lincoln's mother

looking girl, I should say over twenty. . . . We had
bear meat; venison; wild turkey and ducks; eggs, wild

and tame, so common that you could buy them at two bits a bushel; maple-sugar swung on a string; sirup in big gourds; and a sheep that the two families had barbecued whole over coals of wood burned in a pit and covered with green boughs to keep the juice in.''

When the revelings had ended, Mr. Lincoln took his wife to his only home, ''a one-roomed cabin with a huge outside chimney, a single window, and a rude door. They had a cow and calf, milk and butter, and a good feather bed. They had home-woven 'kiver-lids,' big and little pots, a loom and a wheel.'' And though this home may seem rude to us, it sheltered a happy family, for it was not long until two children, Abe and his sister Nancy, came to brighten the fireside.

Mrs. Lincoln was a woman five feet five inches tall, slender, pale of complexion, and sad in expression; but she possessed a heroic nature. She was the teacher of the home. She taught Mr. Lincoln how to read and spell, using her Bible as the text-book, and at her knee Nancy and Abe heard all the Bible lore, fairy tales, and country legends she had been able to gather.

It is said that it was she who inspired Mr. Lincoln to leave the Kentucky home to build up another in the free State of Indiana. And in the fall of 1816 they started by horseback and by wagon on their journey. They settled near Little Pigeon Creek, not far from Gentryville, Ind., at a place now called Lincoln City. There they built a cabin of one room, with a loft above. For a time this house had no window, door, or floor. The furniture was of their own make, of the rudest sort; and Abe's bed was a heap of dry leaves in the corner of the loft. The food was coarse and rudely prepared, but it was usually plentiful. The clothing was scant and home-made, but the family was, for a time, happy.

LINCOLN AND HIS MOTHER

But all too soon a gloom settled upon this home. Mrs. Lincoln became ill, and one morning Abe saw his father make a green-pine box and put his mother into it, for she had died. She was buried under a tree, not far from the cabin home, almost without prayer. But Abe, as young as he was, wrote to a parson in Kentucky all about it and urged him to come and preach her funeral. Three months later the minister arrived and conducted the service which seemed to the child a necessary honor to the dead. Though Abe's earthly relation with his mother was now severed, his affections toward her were never broken. He would often betake himself to the lonely grave and there weep over his irreparable loss.

A few years ago a monument (see the picture) was erected to the memory of this great woman, and a park called the Nancy Hanks Lincoln Park is now set aside.

LINCOLN'S GOOD QUALITIES

LET US notice some of Abraham Lincoln's good qualities. One of these was his respect for his mother, who died when he was about nine years old. He once said, "All that I am, or hope to be, I owe to my mother." She had taught him to read the Bible, and had perhaps taught him the scripture, "Honor thy father and thy mother."

Not only did he love and respect his own mother, but, after his father married again, he loved and respected his stepmother. She said of him, "He never gave me a cross word or look, and never refused, in fact or appearance, to do anything I requested of him."

Another good quality of Lincoln's life was his strict honesty, which caused him to be called "Honest Abe." The story is told that when a boy he borrowed from a neighbor a book, "Life of Washington." He read it at night until the candle burned out, and then he put it between the logs in the loft where he slept. During the night a heavy rain came up, and the book was wet through and through. After drying the book as well as he could, he went and told the neighbor what had happened to the book and offered to work for him to pay the damage. He worked three days pulling corn to pay for it.

Other incidents that show his strict honesty, even in little things, occurred while he was clerking in a store. One evening in counting the cash he found there were a few cents too much and discovered that he had made a mistake in making change for a lady, there being about six cents yet due her. After he closed the store, he

LINCOLN'S GOOD QUALITIES

walked several miles to her home to make the matter right.

At another time, it is said, when he arrived at the store one morning he noticed on the scales a weight that he had used the night before. The weight was not the one that he had intended to use, but was a smaller one. So the purchaser had received two ounces less of tea than had been paid for. Lincoln made this right also.

Then, too, many incidents might be mentioned to show his kindness. Lincoln's strict honesty and great kindness were two of the things that made him great.

"While he and his father's family were moving from Indiana to Illinois, they had a stream of water to cross in weather cold enough to freeze the water's surface. After the family had reached the farther side of the stream, Abraham noticed his little dog standing on the opposite bank and yelping piteously because it was afraid to plunge into the icy water. 'I can't stand that,' said Abraham. 'I can not bear to see even a puppy in distress.' So he rolled up his trousers and waded into the stream, barefooted, took the dog in his arms, and carried it safely over."

"There is still another story illustrating Lincoln's kindness to animals. A friend of his who was one of a company, including Lincoln, traveling one time, relates that after passing through a thicket of wild plum- and crab-apple-trees the company stopped to water their horses. One of the party, who had been riding with Lincoln, came up alone. He was asked, 'Where is Lincoln?' He replied, 'When I saw him last, he had got two birds which the wind had blown out of their nests, and he was hunting for the nest that he might put them back into it.' In a short time Lincoln came up and reported that he had found the nest and restored the birds to their place. The other men laughed at him for taking so much pains with two fledglings, but Lincoln said, 'I could not have slept tonight if I had not restored those little birds to their mother.' "

THE HELEN KELLER OF CHINA

AMONG China's deaf-mutes there is a blind girl who has been called a Chinese Helen Keller. When a small child this girl had smallpox, which left her blind and deaf and dumb. She was sixteen or eighteen years of age when Miss Carter, with the assistance of Mrs. Sen, a graduate of a Chinese high school, took charge of her. She had grown up in absolute ignorance, and at times she would give way to violent outbursts of temper.

To teach her the sign-language and reading and writing was no small task; but, knowing that continued patient effort yields results, these ladies began the work. It took three months to teach her that d-o-l-l, spelled in her hand with the alphabet for the blind, stood for the object placed in her arms. But at last the ideas began to enter her mind, and then the work went easier. By the end of ten months she had learned the Braille system of raised letters.

At the end of two years and a half of training, little Wang Fung-Ying (for this was the girl's name) had made wonderful advancement. A visitor who saw her about that time writes the following:

"A short time after my entrance Fung-Ying was brought to the door, and with little hesitancy she found her way to Miss Carter's side, and held the palm of her hand up to learn what was wanted of her. Miss Carter told her to get her Braille slate and her handkerchief. She did both without the least hesitation.

"While we were talking, Miss Carter spelled in English into Fung-Ying's hand that she was to go out and pick some flowers for the guest. This she did, carefully finding the flowers from among the leaves. When she had picked a large bunch, she brought them into the house, presented them to me, and then took my hands and put the palms together. This is a Chinese greeting or thank you: she wished to show me how to do it.

"A few moments after this, she discovered that she had lost her hair-ribbon among the flowers, and this worried her very much. She wrote in Braille upon her slate, 'Lost my hair-string among the flowers.'"

Miss Carter is teaching her to speak. She learns to make the sound by placing her fingers on her teacher's tongue, lips, and throat, then putting her fingers on her own tongue and giving out the sound according to the position of the tongue. In showing her visitor how she did this, the girl made the sound of several letters. Then as the teacher touched Fung-Ying's hair the girl spoke distinctly the Chinese word *fa,* which means hair.

Seeing what can be accomplished even by those deprived of the senses of sight and hearing is surely an inspiration to us to put forth faithful effort to accomplish something in this life ourselves.

SAINT PATRICK

IF EVER you visit in Ireland, you will hear and see something to remind you of Saint Patrick, the patron saint of Ireland. Though not the first to introduce Christianity into Ireland, he was the first who had any success in what was then a pagan land. He arrived there sometime about the beginning of the fourth century, and his great zeal caused him to soon carry the gospel over all the land. He was a true saint of God, and soon a bright flame of holiness was shining over Ireland. He established schools, which became famous for their learning and high Christian character. Young men from all parts of Europe came to sit at the feet of the learned Christians in Ireland and to take back to their own lands the light that had been kindled in their hearts while they studied there.

While preaching at Tara, the seat of the king of Ireland, St. Patrick is said to have used the shamrock, a small plant of the clover family, as an illustration of the trinity of God. "Three leaves but one stem, three persons but one God," he said, and, from that day to this, the shamrock has been the emblem of Ireland.

Every seventeenth of March, throughout all Ireland, a general holiday is observed in honor of St. Patrick. Then, every Irishman wears a shamrock in his hat, as a remembrance of the man who first preached the gospel to the pagan ancestors of the Irish people.

St. Patrick lived to a good old age. There is much uncertainty as to his burial-place, but some believe it to have been at Downpatrick. Many pilgrims go each year to see his supposed resting-place, and take away some clay from what they regard as a sacred spot.

THE PRESIDENT AND HIS MOTHER

WHAT would you be thinking about if tomorrow you were to be made president of the United States? Here is a story of one of our great presidents, and what he thought about just before he was inaugurated.

He lived near Cleveland, and a few days before the great ceremony, he wrote to his old mother and said, "I want you to go to Washington with me." She was very much surprized, and after thinking it all over, wrote to her son, of whom she was very proud, and said: "I can not go to Washington. I would be quite out of place there among the great people whom you will meet. I'll stay at home and pray for you." He quickly sent the answer, "I'll not go without you," and so together they traveled to the capital city. They went to the same hotel, and when the time came for the ceremony, they went out together, his mother leaning on his arm. They entered the carriage and drove to the Capitol, where a great crowd of over 100,000 people were waiting. It was a gala occasion—the high platform and all the celebrated men from all over the country, governors, judges, and ministers, and the great sea of white faces that were all turned to the one central place, where he was. The people noticed that instead of taking the chair that was provided for him, he gave it to his mother. Then he delivered his inaugural address, and after he had taken the oath to be true to his high office, and before he sat down, he turned and put his arms around his mother and kissed her.

Do you know who he was? He was one of our martyred presidents. His name was James A. Garfield. That was one of the most beautiful things he ever did, and all that great crowd of waiting people, after the din was over and they had gone to their own homes, thought so, too. You know our mothers do for us far more than we can ever repay, and they are more interested in our success than perhaps we are ourselves. None of you should ever get too big, or too old, or go too far away so as to forget Mother or to forget to make her happy in your own happiness. It would be worth while to live in order to do just that.

FLORENCE NIGHTINGALE

THE name of Florence Nightingale is dear to every boy and girl of England. A brief sketch of the life of this noble woman will, no doubt, be interesting to our American boys and girls and, it is hoped, will inspire them with a desire to live for others.

Miss Nightingale was born of wealthy parents, and her home, Lea Hurst, was a place of ideal loveliness. She and her elder sister, Parthenople, lived free, happy lives. Mr. Nightingale favored the higher education of women; and before Florence had reached her seventeenth year she was skilled in science, classics, and mathematics, had a wide acquaintance with standard literature, was a fair artist, a good musician, and could speak French, German, and Italian fluently.

The wealth and social distinction of the family, however, did not allure her to a life of fashion. She possessed social qualities that fitted her for rank in society, but she broke away from the fascination of a life that riches made possible and accepted a routine of duty which the poorest might follow.

From a child she was interested in the poor and sick around her father's estate. She was never happier than when taking food, clothing, or some other gift from her parents to the needy. Her sympathy was not only with human sufferers, but she was tender toward every living thing—insects, birds, cats, dogs, and horses. Her first attempt at nursing was performed on an old Scotch shepherd's dog which had injured its leg.

Her interest in the suffering did not become less as she grew older. She traveled much with her parents

"Making her solitary rounds"

and everywhere they went she wanted to visit the hospitals and jails. She thought young women should be educated to be nurses, and when she was twenty-five, though nursing was then looked upon as a menial occupation, she entered the training-school for nurses at Kaiserswerth on the Rhine. She completed the course in only six months, but applied herself so closely that she was compelled to take a rest. When a year had passed by she undertook the management of an institution for caring for sick and aged governesses. She did much for this institution, but the strain of such heavy work on her delicate constitution became too much, and she had to go again to Lea Hurst for rest. Little did she know the great work the future held for her, but the experiences of the past ten years had prepared her for it, and when the call came she was ready.

While Miss Nightingale was at Lea Hurst for rest, the Crimean War was raging in southeastern Europe. The English, French, and Turks were fighting Russia. Winter had come on, and a severe one, too. The soldiers endured many hardships because of mismanagement. Though they suffered from cold and hunger, yet they fought bravely.

In the hospitals at Scutari three thousand men lay on the bare ground. There were no nurses and only a few doctors to wait upon the sick and wounded; besides, they had no way of procuring what was necessary. A certain writer says: "There were no vessels for water, no utensils of any kind, no soap, towels, or cloths, no hospital clothes; the men lay in their uniforms stiff with gore, . . . their persons covered with vermin." There was plenty of pork and hard biscuits, but no food suitable for the sick. Some of the wounded soldiers died of starvation.

FLORENCE NIGHTINGALE

News of these awful conditions reached England, and the people were greatly stirred. A relief fund was started, and shirts, sheets, blankets, and other necessaries were collected. But the people were not content with sending supplies. They wished to send some one who could bring order out of confusion and make hospitals comfortable for the sick.

Who should this person be? Many thought Florence Nightingale should go, while others thought such a frail woman as she would not survive the exposure one month at the seat of war. It was an experiment to send a woman.

Meanwhile, Miss Nightingale was wondering if she could be of any service—wondered, indeed, if she could go to the relief of the soldiers whose forlorn condition lay as a heavy burden on her heart night and day. She wrote a letter to the Secretary of War offering her services, and it happened that on the very same day the Secretary wrote to her asking her if she would go.

This wealthy, high-born lady was willing to leave her loved ones and her beautiful home, where she was surrounded with every comfort, and go to the East, where she would expose herself to disease, to nurse soldiers, usually considered a rough class; and she would have to face the awful conditions we have described. Why was she willing to do this? For the very reason that she had compassion for the suffering, and compassion that caused her to act.

Miss Nightingale with her thirty-four assistant nurses arrived at Scutari on November 5, on the day the battle of Inkermann was fought. She found so much confusion and misery that a woman with less coolness or executive ability would not have known what to do. The change she brought about in a short time was wonderful. In a few months the death-rate was reduced from sixty to one per cent—all the outcome of proper nursing. The filthy, uncomfortable quarters were changed to neat, clean, attractive apartments. Cheerfulness and hope took the place of sadness and despair.

A writer gives this brief description of the Lady-in-chief: "In the outer room we caught a momentary glimpse of the justly celebrated Miss Nightingale, the fair heroine of Scutari; an amiable and highly intelligent-looking lady of some thirty summers, delicate in form and prepossessing in appearance. Her energies were concentrated for the instant in the careful preparation of a dish of delectable food for an enfeebled patient—one of her homely ministrations to the wan victims of relentless war, for whose relief she so readily and nobly sacrificed the comforts of her quiet, happy English home."

God must have given her special strength. She had to attend thousands of sick men, or see that they were attended. When fresh detachments of wounded came in, she was known to stand for twenty hours at a time, distributing stores, directing nurses, assisting at operations, and ministering to cholera and fever patients.

She saw that the patients were read to, and that there was some one to write letters for them. Much moral and spiritual good she did, also. "When she was shaking up the pillows of poor fellows who were longing for home and loved ones, the most timely and sweetest Christian counsels dropped from her lips, and often proved to be seed sown upon good ground. Many sin-burdened hearts were led in this way to the cross. Many Christian patients were encouraged and strengthened by her life of faith and love; and to them her words were like 'apples of gold in pictures of silver.'"

FLORENCE NIGHTINGALE 103

Another writer says: "When all the medical officers have retired for the night, and silence and darkness have

Florence Nightingale after her return
from the Crimea

settled down on those miles of prostrate sick, she may be observed alone with a little lamp in her hand making her solitary rounds."

Though she had to labor hard, yet one thing made the labor seem light and easy, and that was the respect, affection, and gratitude of the men. They always showed the greatest respect for her. There was an absence of the coarseness she expected to find among the soldiers.

One of the men said of her: "To see her pass was happiness. As she passed down the beds she would nod to one and smile to many more; but she could not do it to all, you know. We lay there by hundreds; but we could kiss her shadow as it fell, and lay our heads upon the pillow again, content."

Only once during her two years' stay in the East was she stricken down with fever. When she recovered she refused to go home for rest, but again took up her work. She continued at her post till the war was over.

England proposed to give her the grandest reception ever accorded a woman, but desiring to avoid such publicity, she took passage on a French steamer under an assumed name and arrived at Lea Hurst before her family knew she had left Scutari. The government, finding that she really did not want to receive a gift of money for her services, presented her with two hundred and fifty thousand dollars with which to found a training-school for nurses.

The fearful physical strain of those two years to her already enfeebled condition caused her a life-long martyrdom of pain. She had to spend the remainder of her life in enforced retirement.

FROM POVERTY TO THE PRESIDENTIAL CHAIR

ON DEC. 29, 1818, in Raleigh, N. C., a boy was born who was déstined to combat successfully with poverty and ignorance and in spite of these hindrances render valuable service to his fellow men. He was named Andrew, and only four years later he was left an orphan by the death of his father.

As the father was a poor man and left no money to his family, Andrew had to face the world without any education, and early support himself by his own labor. At the age of ten years he was apprenticed to Mr. Selby, a tailor.

While working in Mr. Selby's shop, Andrew often had the privilege of hearing a gentleman read to the workmen. The boy became very much interested, and determined to learn to read. He spent all his leisure time in studying. The ability to read proved a great source of satisfaction to him, and he perused such books as he could obtain.

A few months before his apprenticeship expired, he fell into trouble by throwing stones at an old woman's house and ran away to avoid the consequences. But later, he returned, apologized for his misdemeanor, and offered to pay Mr. Selby for the unfulfilled portion of his apprenticeship. Selby, however, required security, which Andrew could not furnish. So he took his mother, who was dependent upon him for support, to Greenville, Tenn., where he put up a shop of his own.

Soon after coming to Greenville he married, and under the instructions of his wife he learned "to write and cypher." He took great interest in local politics, and, when he was twenty-one years old, he organized a party of working men to oppose the aristocratic element that

The old tailor-shop

had always ruled the town. To qualify himself for public speaking, he joined a debating society, which was

FROM POVERTY TO PRESIDENTIAL CHAIR 107

made up of young men of the neighborhood and students of Greenville College. He became a prominent member and won popularity among the students of the college. In speaking of him, one of the students says:

"On approaching the village, there stood on the hill by the highway a solitary little house, perhaps ten feet square. We invariably entered when passing. It contained a bed, two or three stools, and a tailor's platform. Here we delighted to stop, because here lived one whom we knew outside of school, and made us welcome; one who would amuse us by his social good nature, taking more than ordinary interest in catering to our pleasure."

Thus Andrew in his early years endeared himself to the hearts of working men and students. At the age of twenty-two he was elected mayor of the town. At the age of twenty-seven he was elected to the Legislative Assembly, but at the next election he failed to return to the Legislature, having made himself unpopular by opposing a certain bill which became a law. It was not long, however, until his judgment concerning the law proved good, and later he was again chosen a member of the Legislature. Afterward he was sent to the State Senate, then to Congress, and he finally filled the presidential chair as Andrew Johnson.

When the Southern States seceded, Johnson did all he could to restore Tennessee to the Union. His life was often endangered, and at one time his family was thrown out of their home and his nine slaves were confiscated, yet he was firm to his conviction that the Union should be upheld at all hazards. He was appointed military governor of Tennessee during the war, and was elected vice-president of the United States at Lincoln's second election.

After Johnson became president on account of Lincoln's death, he had a very hard place to fill. And because he failed to be as severe with the Southern States as Congress desired, he came near being thrown out of office. A few months before his term of office expired, he issued a full pardon to everybody who had participated in the rebellion, thus showing his good feeling toward all his countrymen. He was succeeded in the presidential office by Ulysses S. Grant, after which he retired to his home in Greenville, Tenn. His countrymen have showed their love and respect for him by erecting on top of a beautiful hill just outside the city a monument to his memory.

A BLIND GIRL WHO BECAME FAMOUS
Part I

NESTLED among the beautiful hills of New York nearly a century ago was the home of a little blind girl who was to become one of the greatest and most widely-known hymn-writers of the present day—Fanny Crosby. Her long life of usefulness, which expired near the close of her ninety-fifth year (Feb. 12, 1915), is full of interest to the thousands who have sung her inspiring hymns and thereby partaken of her noble spirit.

At a very early age her eyesight became affected, which resulted in permanent blindness. But through all the long years of physical darkness that followed, her perseverance in her one ambition—to fill some little place of usefulness in God's great world—is worthy of note.

As a child, although blind, Fanny was by no means helpless, but indulged in many of the sports enjoyed by the other children. Of herself she says, "I could climb a tree, or ride a horse, as well as any of them; and many good people, when seeing me at play, were surprized to learn of my misfortune."

One of her favorite pastimes was to listen to the many voices of nature—"the laughing and sighing of the wind; the sobbing of the storm; the rippling of water; the rain on the roof; the artillery of the thunder"—which served their places well in furnishing wholesome entertainment for their little friend.

The fact that she was deprived of her eyesight did not hinder her youthful imagination from carrying her far up in the heights of fame and honor. But this question often puzzled her, "How am I ever to realize my ambitions?" In reply to her many and eager questionings she so often heard: "Oh, you can not do this —because you are blind, you know." "You can never go there, because it would not be worth while: you could not see anything if you did, you know." How many of us, if we should encounter such discouragements, would persevere in our undertakings? Perhaps the secret of Fanny's sweet, undaunted disposition lay in the fact that very early in life she had learned of Him who "knoweth our frame," and "remembereth that we are dust." Often, when depressed feelings came over her, she would steal off alone, kneel down, and there pray to her heavenly Father, who seemed to assure her that some day she would be happy and useful, even though she was blind. Then she would go back among her associates, cheered and encouraged with the feeling that the time would soon come when her life would be filled with activity and usefulness.

When ten years old Fanny Crosby had memorized the first four books of both the Old and New Testaments, and many poems besides. Her love for poetry had become manifest at an early age. Often she wondered who wrote the beautiful hymns she heard sung, and whether she herself could ever make hymns that people would sing. The following lines she composed when only eight years old:

> "Oh, what a happy child I am,
>   Although I can not see!
> I am resolved that in this world
>   Contented I will be.
>
> "How many blessings I enjoy
>   That other people don't.
> So weep or sigh because I'm blind;
>   I can not, nor I won't!"

Other verses followed, always on subjects that appealed to her most; and by and by, becoming eager to know what other people would think of her rhymes, she began repeating them to her mother. This resulted in a number of them being written, and copies being sent to her grandfather, who at once became her "gallant and unqualified admirer." He, however, cautioned her mother not to tell her of her wonderful ability, lest it instill pride into her heart and spoil her. But, upon seeing her soon afterward, he could not refrain from telling her himself!

Then the terrible hunger for knowledge, that afflicted her during those years, became intensified. Night after night she went to bed drearily, weeping because she could not drink of the waters of knowledge that she knew were surging all around. "I felt at times like a soldier on a great lake of fresh, crystal water," she said, "heated and thirsty, but bound hand and foot so that he could not get to the blessed relief. 'Dear God, please give me light!' was my prayer day by day. I did not mean physical light, but mental. I had long been contented to bear the burden of blindness, but my education—my education—how was I to get it? The ordinary schools could do little for me; I was not able to read and educate myself, as many home-students have done; those around had little time to read to me; and I felt as if I were in danger of becoming more ignorant every day. God help those who thirst for knowledge, and find every way for obtaining it cut off!"

Part II

"IF THE founders and sustainers of institutions for the blind could only know a millionth part of the joy they cause, they would feel repaid for their money and their efforts again and again"—these were **Fanny** Crosby's sentiments.

At the age of fifteen she experienced the thrill of joy that comes to waiting souls when at last they realize the answer to their prayers. She was informed that arrangements had been made for her to attend the school for the blind in New York. The necessary preparations in those days were few and simple, and soon after the delightful information had been imparted to her, she was on her way to New York. Here she was kindly received by the superintendent of the institution, and welcomed into what meant to her a new world.

All went well at first, with exceptional attacks of homesickness now and then. But soon there loomed up before her, like some great monster, a difficulty in the form of arithmetic. How she loathed the science of numbers! But, with her usual perseverance, she realized that this great foe to her peace of mind had to be conquered, so to conquer it she began. The only alleviation of the miseries brought on by the multiplication table was the swinging, rhymeless motion which it suggested to her mind. Among her other studies were grammar, philosophy, astronomy, and political economy, all of which she enjoyed very much. The lessons were given in the form of lectures and readings, and the pupils' standing in the school depended much upon their ability to remember and recite these lessons.

During the first part of her school-life Fanny composed several little poems from time to time, which were received with great favor, both by teachers and fellow pupils. This gave rise to a feeling of self-gratification, which naturally produced some outward manifestations. One day the superintendent called her to his office, and she, supposing he was desiring a new ode or other **kind**

A BLIND GIRL WHO BECAME FAMOUS 113

of lyric, went readily enough. Imagine her surprize at his first few words: "Fanny, your—your *attempts* at poetry have brought you into prominence here in the school, and a great deal of flattery has been the result. Shun a flatterer, Fanny, as you would a snake!" He went on to say that as yet she knew very little about poetry, or, in fact, anything else—compared with what there was to be known. And he advised her not to think too much about rhymes and the praises that come from them; but, rather, to store her mind with more useful knowledge, and to think more of what she could *be* than of how she could *appear*.

Speaking of the interview, she says, "His words were bomb-shells in the camp of my self-congratulatory thoughts; but they did me an immense amount of good. Something said to me, 'He tells the truth, Fanny, and it is all for your own benefit.' Still, the hot tears came to my eyes, as perhaps they would have done to those of any ambitious girl; and I naturally felt much pain and mortification at his words. But a reaction of feeling soon took place; and going around behind his chair, and putting my arms around his neck, I kissed him on the forehead. 'You have talked to me as my father would have talked, were he living,' I said, 'and I thank you for it over and over again. You have given me a lesson that I might have had to learn through bitter experience, and I shall profit by it.'"

And through the years that followed she proved that she had indeed taken this lesson to heart and had received a lasting benefit from it.

Among her pleasant school memories were the vacation periods. These she always spent at home, where she found a royal reception awaiting her from her little sisters. They gathered flowers of every kind for her, saved bits of candy for weeks prior to her home-coming, and planned delightful excursions into the woods. And the questions they would ask! She was requested to describe every scholar, and teacher, and to tell of every distinguished visitor who had favored the institution with a call. Also, she was required to recite every poem she had composed since her previous visit at home, and to subject the same to their criticism—which, it is needless to say, rather bordered on enthusiasm, for, to their mind, "Sister Fan" was the greatest poet of ancient or modern times!

Part III

AT THE age of twenty-two Fanny Crosby was considered competent to teach grammar, rhetoric, and ancient and modern history, and she became one of the regular teachers of the Institution.

While preparing for this position, however, she was constantly tempted to turn her attention into the pursuit of her increasing ambition to write poetry. But the superintendent still seemed in doubt as to the wisdom of encouraging her in this pursuit. Finally he talked long with her on the subject, told her that many people wrote rhymes because they were poetry-lovers rather than poets, and gently but firmly forbade her "producing any more of the dangerous article for three months." This seemed like a severe method of uncalled for punishment; but feeling sure that the superintendent knew what was best for her, she acquiesced, and avoided a rhyme as she would have avoided the measles.

Soon afterward, however, Dr. Combe, a distinguished phrenologist of Scotland, came to her rescue. During his visit to the Institution, several of the students sub-

A BLIND GIRL WHO BECAME FAMOUS 115

mitted to his examination. When Fanny's turn came, upon examining her head, he exclaimed, "Why, here is a poet! Give her every advantage that she can have; let her hear the best books and converse with the best writers, and she will make her mark in the world." That converted the superintendent, who, on the following morning, informed Fanny that she could write as much poetry as she wished. Then she was encouraged to study all the intricacies of verse, and to become a first-class writer.

During her experience as student and instructor Fanny Crosby was privileged to meet many distinguished persons. Among the first of these were William Cullen Bryant, the best-known American poet at that time, and Horace Greeley, the celebrated American journalist, author, and politician. Others who visited the Institution were Henry Clay, the great orator; General Winfield Scott, a hero of the Mexican War; President Polk; and General Henri Gratien Bertrand, Napoleon's faithful marshall.

While in Washington, D. C., in 1844, where she had gone with others to awaken public attention in favor of the blind, she was invited to deliver a poetical address before a most distinguished audience, consisting of both the Senate and the House of Representatives. She was the first poet ever invited to speak, or to recite his or her own productions, before the great National Assembly. Among those in the audience were John Quincy Adams, James Buchanan, Andrew Johnson, Hannibal Hamlin, Stephen A. Douglas, Jefferson Davis, and Alexander Stephens. She visited Washington, D. C., and again addressed Congress in 1847.

In 1843 she and several others from the school visited Niagara Falls. Of her experience there she says: "As we stood upon Goat Island, and one of our teachers described Horseshoe Falls and other famous localities in his view, I could almost fancy I heard the morning stars singing together, and the sons of God shouting for joy! I could hear the trumpet voice of this king of cataracts proclaiming the power of the almighty Hand; I could feel the fresh breezes that spring from the bosom of the whirling waters; I could (sweetest thought of all) enjoy the enjoyment of my friends who could see, and listen to their animated descriptions. Indeed, I sometimes think that blind people see more than their friends who have the power of vision; for they get descriptions from various points of view, that it is not considered necessary to give those who can look for themselves.''

Part IV

WHEN on her trip to Niagara Falls, Fanny Crosby met at Oswego, N. Y., a blind boy just about to enter the years of manhood. His name was Alexander Van Alstyne. His mother desired to send him to the Institution for the Blind in New York City, and requested that he be placed under Fanny's personal charge. To this she consented as a teacher of the Institution, little dreaming of the outcome.

During the four years he remained in the Institution he was in several of her classes. In 1848 he graduated, then went to Union College, Schenectady, where he studied Greek, Latin, and theology, distinguishing himself by his scholarship. In 1855 he came back to New York City, and for two years taught in the Institution for the Blind. The following year he and Fanny Crosby were married. At his request her literary name re-

A BLIND GIRL WHO BECAME FAMOUS 117

mained unchanged, and for this reason we know of her today as Fanny Crosby rather than as Mrs. Alexander Van Alstyne.

The most important work of her life, so far as poetry is concerned, began in 1864. In that year she was introduced to Wm. B. Bradbury, who was already famous as a writer of hymn-music. Mr. Bradbury insisted that she write for him, and that she begin at once. Her first hymn to which he set the music was the one that begins:

> "We are going, we are going
> To a home beyond the skies,
> Where the roses never wither,
> And the sunlight never dies."

For four years they worked together; then Mr. Bradbury died. At his funeral the first hymn sung was that one with which they had commenced their work.

Among the other writers of hymn-music who assisted Fanny Crosby after Mr. Bradbury's death were W. H Doane, Ira B. Sankey, Prof. H. R. Palmer, and Hubert P. Main.

One day while she was writing hymns for Mr. Doane, he came hurriedly to her, and said, "Fanny, I have just forty minutes to catch the cars for Cincinnati; during that time you must write me a hymn, and give me a few minutes to catch the train." He hummed the melody to which he wanted the words written, and in fifteen minutes she had written the words and handed them to him. When he returned from Cincinnati, he published them; and now that hymn is sung wherever Christian music is known. It begins thus: "Safe in the arms of Jesus."

A bit of Fanny Crosby's personal experience, which led to the writing of the hymn "All the Way My

Savior Leads Me," is interesting. One day she needed five dollars for a particular purpose, and not knowing just how to get it, she was impressed to pray for it. Not long after she had prayed for the money, a gentleman came to the house, shook hands with her and exchanged a few words, then went out immediately. When she closed her hand after the friendly salutation, she found in it a five-dollar bill which he had left there. Her first thought was, "In what a wonderful way the Lord helps me! All the way my Savior leads me!" Immediately afterward she wrote the hymn, for which Dr. Robert Lowry supplied music.

After her husband's death, in 1902, Fanny Crosby removed to Bridgeport, Conn., where she spent the last years of her life in restful retirement. She continued to write in her old days. In all, she wrote more than six thousand hymns, many of which have made their way all over the world, and have become universal favorites. Some have been translated into many other languages.

She expressed a desire to reach the age of 103—the age at which her grandmother died—but in this connection, she said, "Whenever the Lord calls me, I am willing to go; but if he chooses to leave me here until I reach 'my mark,' or even longer, I shall continue to gather sheaves till the sun goes down, and to sing and write hymns to his praise."

A GREAT MAN WHO LOVED HIS MOTHER

IT WAS the closing day of the commencement in a college of high standing. Not only were the diplomas to be given to the graduates, but a gold medal was to be presented to the one who had made the best record. When the time came for the medal to be presented, the audience waited in almost breathless expectancy, to learn who the fortunate one should be.

The members of the class also were eagerly waiting to hear the decision of the judges. They felt sure that the honor would go either to the brilliant son of a certain wealthy lawyer, or to a certain diligent and studious young man, who, though poor, had made the very best of the opportunities afforded him. They were satisfied when the latter was awarded the honor.

But how did the young man feel? Did he think he had done something worthy of this honor? He thought of a little, bent figure of a woman seated in the audience. Going to her, he placed the medal upon her and said, "Mother, you are the one who has earned this medal, by your faithful labor and sacrifice." Surely that mother felt repaid for the many days and nights of toil that it required to keep her son in school. And her son showed true appreciation for her efforts.

Another excellent example of filial love is found in the life of the "father of his country," George Washington. Not only did he manifest this in his affection for his parents, but also in strict obedience to the principles and truths which they taught him. They had taken care to plant in his heart, when a child, the seeds of truth, honesty, and love for God and the right.

120 BITS OF BIOGRAPHY

Washington's visit to his mother

Throughout his life these bore fruit, making him a strong, noble character. How beautiful was his devotion to his mother even after he became a man crowned with fame and honor!

Let us try to imagine his joy when, as a lad, his much-desired hope of becoming a midshipman on a British man-of-war was about to become a reality. After long and earnest pleadings his brother Lawrence had at last gained his mother's consent for him to go. And now his trunk is packed and carried on board the ship that is to take him so far from home. But before leaving he must go and bid farewell to his loved ones. As he approaches his mother to tell her good-by, she loses her usual self-control, and begins to weep.

"I can not consent to let you go," she says, "it will break my heart, George."

The boy is much affected by the sight of his mother's grief. The new life and the hope of rising to a place of honor fail to outweigh his regard for his mother's comfort, and he says, "Mother, I can never go and cause you so much grief. I will stay at home."

This decision was not kept without some disappointment on his part, but he was happier in yielding to his mother's reasonable request than he would have been in gratifying his own wishes.

Later on in life he showed the same love and tenderness toward his mother. After he had been elected president of the United States he paid a farewell visit to his mother before going to the capitol to take up his public duties. As she was very old and was suffering from a serious disease, both of them seemed to recognize the fact that they should never meet again on earth. It was a very touching scene, and has been described by a friend in the following words:

"Washington was deeply affected. His head rested upon the shoulder of his parent, whose aged arm feebly, yet fondly, encircled his neck. That brow on which fame had wreathed the purest laurel virtue ever gave to created man, relaxed from its lofty bearing. That look was bent in filial tenderness upon the time-worn features of the aged matron. He wept. A thousand recollections crowded upon his mind, as memory carried him back to the old mansion and the days of childhood, where he beheld that mother, whose care, education, and discipline caused him to reach the topmost height of praiseworthy ambition. Yet how were his glories forgotten while he gazed upon her, whom, wasted by time and malady, he should part with to meet no more!"

LUDWIG VAN BEETHOVEN

IN READING about men who have been really great, there is something that reminds us that "we can make our lives sublime." One thing to be noticed, especially of eminent men, is their close application to their work, and their hard work. Beethoven was no exception to the rule.

His ancestors were from Belgium. His grandfather Louis, or Ludwig, Van Beethoven, went to Germany in 1732 and settled near Bonn. He was soon recognized as a musician, and for his beautiful voice was chosen by the archbishop to sing tenor with the court musicians. His son, Johann, inherited the same talent, and held the same position. Johann married the daughter of the cook at the Elector's palace, and to them was born Ludwig, the greatest musician in many ways that ever was known. His originality has never been, and great masters say it never can be, surpassed. He is to the musical world what Shakespeare is to the poetical world. His achievements are the highest in classical symphony.

In his youth he suffered from mistreatments of a drunken and shiftless father, who decided, upon discovering his son had some talent, to make of him a prodigy. When but four years old he was set to arduous study for hours upon violin and piano, which caused a strain upon his nervous system that he never fully overcame.

When but eleven years old he was employed as assistant organist, and when but fourteen was appointed second court organist with a salary. When seventeen his career really began. Some music-lovers began to aid him and his family, for he was compelled to assist in its support. These friends paid his expenses to Vienna, where he visited the great master, Mozart, who whispered to his friends, "Mark him well, some day he will make a stir in the world." He spent most of his life in and around Vienna. It became his permanent home. But once he was called to Bonn to the death-bed of his much beloved mother, who through all his hardships had been gentle and kind. He was detained there for some time, to help in the support of the family by giving music lessons and concerts.

He made friends possibly more through his genius than otherwise, as he was generally uncommunicative and a little abrupt. Among his closest friends and benefactors was Count Waldstein. Later he studied music under Hayden and Albrechtsen. One characteristic that annoyed his teachers was his preference for acquiring by his own toilsome experience what would have been easier to have accepted on the authority of others. It was probably through this method that he discovered his new order of music.

He always maintained a certain independence of character. Once when the Van in his name was alluded to as a mark of nobility, he touched first his head and then his heart, exclaiming, "My patent of nobility is here, and here."

Some one submitted a manuscript to him, meekly suggesting that it was "with God's help," to which he replied, "O man, help thyself." Do not infer from this that he was not religious, for he was devout; but he was also self-reliant.

His great impulses that conceived most of his grandest works were received during his lonely walks while in communion with nature. We say "lonely walks," for

LUDWIG VAN BEETHOVEN

before he was forty years old, and when just at the height of his ability, he became stone deaf. He had known for years that he was becoming deaf and it added great sorrow to his life, but with a powerful will he grappled with fate, determined that it should not take away his talent. While he was capable through the art of sound of softening the mood and ushering in quietness and rest to the spirits of others, yet he was deprived of receiving the same blessings to himself. Though bereft of the dearest thing in the world to him—the charms of the art of sound—he pours forth to the world his aspirations in a sublime benediction.

He wanted to revel in sympathy. He wanted to be loved. He wanted companionship; but instead he was compelled to isolate himself and live as a hermit. He tried to lavish his love upon a nephew, the son of a brother who died. But the nephew proved a miserable scapegrace, to the bitter disappointment of his benefactor. Beethoven's life from one side might be described as of one overtaxed and mistreated through unkindness and poverty in youth, and later deprived of life's comforts and pleasures through deafness and misdirected sacrifices. This story, however, would not be complete; for in his soul there dwelt that something that lifted him above his environment, and shed, in its sublime greatness, great joy to the world. His unconsciousness of his greatness may be somewhat realized by this illustration:

Once during the recital of one of his great symphony compositions, the ovation was so great that a policeman was called in to quiet the people. He knew absolutely nothing about it until one of the singers turned him around. The audience, touched by the pathos of the scene, broke into tears and acclamations of sympathy.

His dying words were: "I shall hear in heaven."

FROM PLOW TO MISSION-FIELD

FIJI is not only a "gem in the British crown, but a precious jewel in the missionary diadem, and to John Hunt, above all other men, belongs the honor of having it placed there."

Mr. Hunt was born and reared in England. Though a plow-boy and often laughed at by fellow laborers as being a simpleton, he meditated great things. Hero stories of the open sea caused him to decide secretly, within his own soul, that some day he would be a hero too. But the heroism to which he attained was far different from what he, in his boyhood dreams, imagined.

At the age of nineteen he was fortunate enough to be hired by a farmer who was a reading man. Up to this time John had had no books but the Bible and Pilgrim's Progress, but now, having access to books, he gave all of his spare time to reading and improving himself. As he studied he gradually felt the awakening of powers within him, and one day in the absence of a local preacher he was asked to address the congregation. Some who heard him realized that John Hunt was no common man, and soon he was sent to an institution at Hoxton, where he made rapid progress in his studies.

He turned his attention toward Africa as his future field of usefulness, and his daily prayer was for "fitness for the work of God in that dark continent."

In 1838, about the time English missionaries had stirred English churches with the plea, "Pity poor Fiji," Mr. Hunt was one day summoned to the mission house, and asked whether he would go to Fiji. The ques-

FROM PLOW TO MISSION-FIELD 127

tion startled him, and he asked time to consider. His emotions were deeply stirred. For six years he had loved a girl, Hannah Summers by name, and he was

Natives of Fiji

sure he could never obtain her consent to go amid the perils of cannibalism and paganism he would have to face. But an immediate reply to the letter he wrote her quieted all fears, for she said she was willing to go with him anywhere.

On March 6 of the same year he was married, and on April 29 he and his wife sailed for Sydney, Australia, landing at Fiji December 22. The young couple took up residence among a savage people, but, undismayed, began to learn the language.

Of the horrible conditions existing among the natives, Mr. Hunt said "the half had not been told." The King and one or two of the chiefs were favorable, but their motives were mixed. When asked if they believed Christianity to be true, "True? Everything that comes from white man's country is true; muskets and gunpowder are true; your religion must be true," was the reply. But the power of truth soon began to tell, and there were some real conversions, also real persecutions.

At the end of seven months it was thought best that Mr. and Mrs. Hunt leave this island for Somosomo, the most terrible of the Fiji group, and where any white people who dared to venture were murdered. But there the heroic missionary with his wife, together with another brave couple, went. Their reception was cold and heartless, but there they labored for three years with little apparent results.

Leaving Somosomo they went to Viwa, where Mr. Hunt spent his last six years. This was the most important center in Fiji, and some converts had already been made under another missionary. However, Mr. Hunt's position was a perilous one. But, undaunted, he went on, now translating the New Testament into the Fijian language, now traveling and everywhere making known the glad news of salvation, now organizing schools and training teachers from his most promising converts. He always saw the bright side of everything.

FROM PLOW TO MISSION-FIELD

He could observe a spot of sunlight when others could see nothing but clouds.

Finally the Queen, and the King's personal friend, Veraini, were converted. Veraini became a preacher, and soon the converts to Christianity numbered in the thousands. The great reaction that followed the revival, and the demands made upon Hunt by a settled Christian population, began to tell on him, and his pale face and failing appetite showed to the natives that he was dying. The Christians met and entreated God to spare him to them. Veraini's prayer was: "O Lord, we know that we have been very evil! but spare thy servant! If one must die, take me! take ten of us! but spare thy servant to preach Christ to the people."

It was not to be, and John Hunt, with triumph on his lips, left them on Oct. 4, 1848, at the age of thirty-six years.

LIFE-STORY OF D. L. MOODY

D. L. MOODY'S life, like that of John Wesley's, was largely influenced by the godly example and teaching of his mother, who was a Puritan, of Northfield, Mass. Dwight Lyman was the sixth among seven children. When only four years old he was bereft of his father, who died a bankrupt, leaving the poor wife and seven children at the mercy of their creditors. Dwight's oldest brother was then only thirteen. Neighbors said that one woman could not bring up seven boys, and advised the heart-broken mother to put her children out in homes. But the mother answered, "Not as long as I have these two hands." There was never a more true or devoted mother. Her sorrows only drove her oftener to Jesus' feet. During the first year following her husband's death, she cried herself to sleep every night. But she did not let her children see anything but cheerfulness. Despite the poverty and hardships, she succeeded in making home the sweetest spot on earth to the Moody children. In return for the mother's love and sacrifice for them, the children loved and helped her.

Dwight's boyhood days were about the same as those of the ordinary New England boy. He went to school during the winter and "hired out" during the summer. The very first thing he did to earn money was to drive a neighbor's cows out to pasture on a mountain near by, and he received a cent a day.

When Dwight was only sixteen he proved his ability as a debater, leader, and public speaker. You may be surprized to learn that he did not show much inclination toward spiritual things up to this time, though his

LIFE-STORY OF D. L. MOODY 131

mother was a very religious woman, and faithfully instructed her children in the ways of the Lord. She made it a rule to have the children always attend Sunday-school.

"Nothing that is known of his boyhood gives any reason to expect the large things that followed in Mr. Moody's life. But his love of harmless fun, his keen appreciation of a joke (even upon himself), his sensitive, compassionate nature, and his leadership of his comrades, were features which remained with him throughout the years that followed."

When Dwight became about seventeen years old he longed to be where he could have more privileges. Leaving Northfield, he went to Boston, where he worked as a store-boy for two of his uncles in the shoe business. Though a rough, unpolished country-lad, Dwight was naturally bright and witty, and won many friends. He applied himself to his work, thus proving himself valuable to his employers. His uncles insisted that he attend Sunday-school. He was always courteous and attentive to his teachers. It was through a personal talk of his Sunday-school teacher, while he was at work in the store, that Dwight first became converted. Young Moody was at once very zealous for his Master. The first thought that came to his mind was, "What can I do for Him who has done so much for me?"

At the age of nineteen Dwight left Boston for Chicago, where he earned thirty dollars a week from the very first, in a boot- and shoe-store. Here he again became popular through his ability as a salesman, especially among the rougher class of customers. He had a special knack in handling cross and irritable people.

Now that he was converted, he no longer had to be urged to attend Sunday-school. But he, was not contented to enjoy it by himself; his heart went out to the many young men in the city whom he knew attended neither church nor Sunday-school. He spent a great deal of his spare time visiting boarding-houses and hotels

D. L. Moody

in search of friendless ones, also in distributing tracts. Might not young Moody's example be a good one for the boys to follow today?

Being told by the superintendent of a Sunday-school that he was welcome to teach a class if he could work one up of his own, Dwight immediately set to work, and the next Sunday appeared with eighteen dirty, ragged urchins from the street. While very busy in the city

Dwight often thought of home and mother, and regularly sent letters to her.

Dwight was twenty-four when the Civil War broke out. It was at this time that he felt he should give up business and devote all his time to the work of saving souls. It was one of the hardest struggles of his life, and although he never received a regular salary after that, he never regretted his decision. His brother Warren enlisted and this turned the sympathy of young Moody toward the soldiers. Writing to his mother in the year 1862, he said, "I am holding meetings at the camp every night with the soldiers. A good many of them are turning from the errors of their ways. Mother, I wish you would talk to Warren about his soul. Tell him not to play cards, for it leads to gambling, and gambling leads to hell."

Many were the hours young Moody spent in the boys' tents, praying and singing with them. He often had the privilege of going to the front and ministering to the wounded and the dying, and pointing them to Christ. This kind of work proved of great value to him in his future. From these experiences young Moody gathered a great number of incidents and anecdotes which proved very useful to him in preparing sermons later.

In 1870 occurred the meeting of Moody with Sankey, the great singer. They continued to be coworkers for many years. It was through the influence of Moody that Mr. Sankey was persuaded to give up his position and devote his whole life to the work of telling the gospel in song. The souls won to God through the singing of this man can not be numbered. Speaking of the value of singing, Moody once said, "If you have singing that reaches the heart, it will fill the church every time."

It was one night while Mr. Moody was preaching in Farewell Hall that the great Chicago fire occurred. Before daybreak his home, the hall in which he had just been preaching, and also his church were laid in ashes.

By the year 1875 Moody had returned from his third visit to England. As his Chicago home had been burned, he decided to locate where he could be near his mother in her old age. By this time Northfield had become a great educational center, owing to the many schools, conferences, and other institutions which he had established. During the summer Mr. Moody generally arose about daybreak. It was his custom to spend the early morning hours in prayer and studying the Bible. He claimed that one who followed that plan could not get more than twenty-four hours away from God. During the seasons when the schools were in session, he usually conducted the chapel exercises. It is said that he did the work of about ten men. But in spite of his many cares and responsibilities, Moody took time for relaxation. He was especially fond of caring for the chickens and garden, for he enjoyed seeing things grow.

In 1892 he took a much-needed vacation and made a visit to the Holy Land. On his return trip occurred one of the most thrilling experiences of his life, for he narrowly escaped death by shipwreck. The nervous strain that was undergone by those seven hundred passengers during the eight days and nights of peril was too great for words. Even to Mr. Moody, who had no fear of death, it was one of the darkest hours of his life, for the thought of leaving his family and the work of God, which lay so close to his heart, was almost more than he could bear. Yet he said, "God's will be done." A wonderful deliverance was wrought by God, and Mr. Moody safely reached shore. Upon reaching Northfield he was greeted by the cries and cheers of hundreds of students and friends.

Just before reaching her ninety-second birthday, Mr. Moody's beloved mother passed away. A few months before his mother's death, Mr. Moody had the joy of being a grandfather for the first time. Little Irene helped to fill up the vacancy that was left in his heart. But his joy was not unmixed with pain, for soon his first grandchild and also his namesake were called above. He had been an exceptionally devoted grandfather and these two deaths brought deep sorrow to his heart.

Mr. Moody's last evangelistic-trip was made when he was at the age of sixty-two years. Though compelled to spend most of his last days within his own room, no murmur escaped the lips of this noble man. He continued to plan for the future and fully expected to be well again. He was not tired of life, for he had experienced the great joy of living and working for God; but he was ready and willing to go.

Some of his last words were: "Earth recedes; heaven opens before me." "If this is death, it is sweet! There is no valley here! God is calling me, and I must go!" Sublime indeed were his farewell messages to his loved ones. He talked on and on, speaking as if from another world. He gave directions regarding the carrying on of his work, his school plans, etc. Seeming to see inside of heaven, he exclaimed, "This is my triumph; this is my coronation day! I have been looking forward to it for years." Suddenly a halo of glory was seen to illume his countenance, and in his joy he cried, "Dwight! Irene! I see the children's faces!" Reviving from a severe sinking-spell he said, "No pain! No valley! If this is death, it's not bad at all. It's sweet!" A second and still a third sinking-spell, and he who loved his Redeemer so well on earth passed away to be in His presence forever.

His was a life wholly spent for God, and though he is now silent in death his words and deeds live on and on, inspiring us who study his life with a desire to imitate him in his close walk with God.

> "Lives of great men all remind us
>   We can make our lives sublime,
> And departing, leave behind us
>   Footprints on the sands of time;
> Footprints that perhaps another,
>   Sailing o'er life's solemn main,
> A forlorn and sinsick brother,
>   Seeing, may take heart again."

OUR OWN HELEN KELLER

MOST children have read or heard something about Helen Keller, that famous American girl who can neither see nor hear and yet has obtained a good education.

When we learn of Helen Keller's remarkable achievements, we seeing and hearing girls are almost put to shame. One writer, after speaking of what Helen Keller had done, said, "Yet, here is a girl who 'can't' learn her music, another who 'can't' sew a straight seam, one who 'can't' learn a speech, and hundreds of thousands who 'can't' do this or that; yet while they sit and pout and fret and 'can't,' there is one in their midst, a girl, too, who has even to feel of the human face to catch a smile, or touch the lips to understand a word, but who takes one of the highest places in the world. Helen Keller has met no obstacle too great, no trial too difficult." Girls, and boys, too, let us not be so quick to say "can't."

Helen Keller has gone to college with hearing and seeing girls. She has studied algebra, geometry, physics, history, literature, philosophy, English, French, German, Latin, and Greek. She enjoys reading German and French literature and even the Greek Iliad and Odyssey. She has read the Bible through, and she says she loves it as she loves no other book. Now, if you can imagine yourself unable to see and unable to hear, you can readily see that Helen Keller had many difficulties to overcome.

She communicates with others by the manual alphabet (the letters made by the deaf and dumb in conversation), or she listens to another by holding her fingers over the lips of the speaker. She reads raised print for the blind.

138 BITS OF BIOGRAPHY

She has even learned to speak. This seems very remarkable when we remember that she can not hear a word nor see the movements of the lips when others speak. To

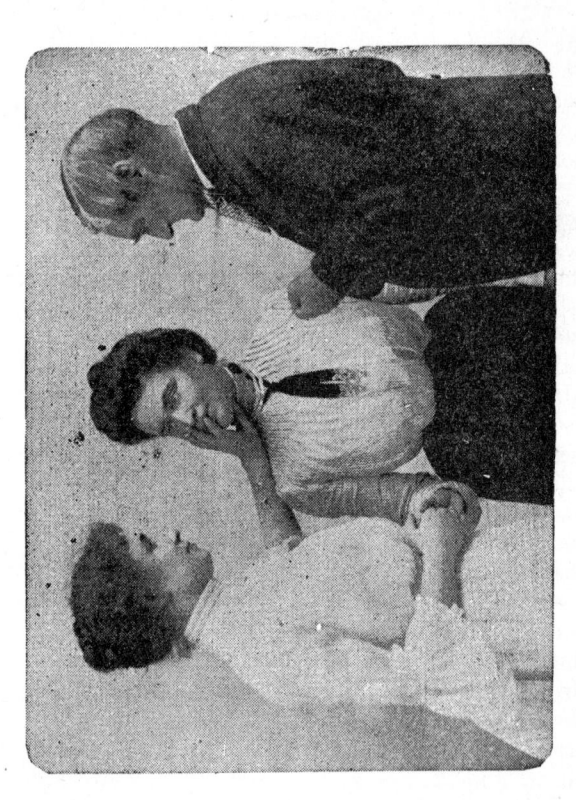

Helen Keller, when a young woman, listening to her teacher, Miss Sullivan, by putting her finger on Miss Sullivan's lips

learn to speak was about the most discouraging thing she undertook, but, as she said, every struggle ends in victory. She says; "No deaf child who has earnestly tried

OUR OWN HELEN KELLER 139

to speak the words which he has never heard—to come out of the prison of silence, where no tone of love, no songs of birds, no strains of music ever pierce the stillness—can forget the thrilling of surprize, the joy of discovery which came to him when he uttered his first word.''

Helen Keller is cheerful and happy. It would be a great blessing to the world if all the seeing and hearing persons were as happy as she. She enjoys things that other people do, though much that we enjoy through our senses of sight and hearing, she must enjoy through her sense of touch.

She very much enjoys a walk in the country. She loves to ride her tandem bicycle, to swim, to take her friends rowing. She enjoys canoeing by moonlight especially. Nothing pleases her more than a frolic with children. Strange as it seems, museums and art stores are sources of pleasure to her. She wonders if she does not enjoy sculpture more with her hand than others do with the eye.

At the age of thirteen she made her first visit to Niagara Falls. It seems strange that she should be impressed with the wonders and beauties of Niagara. But she wrote to her mother, "You can never imagine how I felt when I stood in the presence of Niagara." She wished she could describe the cataract as it was, its beauty and awful grandeur.

Not long after her visit to Niagara she went to the World's Fair. She was given permission to touch the exhibits, and it was said, "Helen sees more with her fingers than we do with our eyes."

Probably some of you are wondering whether Helen Keller was always so unfortunate, whether she never in her life saw her mother's face or heard her voice.

She was born in 1880 in Tuscumbia, a little town of northern Alabama. She was a dear bright baby, much like other babies. But her happy days did not last long. When she was only nineteen months old, the illness came that closed her eyes and ears. The disease was called acute congestion of the stomach and brain. Poor little Helen was left in a dark, silent world.

She became used to the silence and darkness and forgot that it had ever been different. She soon felt the need of communicating with others and began to use crude signs. A shake of the head meant "No," and a nod, "Yes," a pull meant "Come," and a push, "Go." If she wanted bread she imitated the acts of cutting bread and buttering it. If she wanted ice-cream, she would make the sign for working the freezer and shiver. Her mother was able to make her understand many things.

When she was only five years old, she learned to fold and put away the clean clothes, and she knew which were her own. She understood much of what was going on around her. She often went to the garden and loved to smell the flowers. She would wander along the hedge, and guided by the sense of smell would find the first violets of the spring. In the household was little Martha Washington, a daughter of one of the servants. With this girl Helen liked to play.

Poor Helen could hear no tender, loving words. She could not be taught how to be good or what love is. She would let no one kiss her but her mother. She would not respond to caresses. When Christmas came, she enjoyed the pleasant odors and the sweets, but she could not be told the beautiful Christmas story. Her untaught hands destroyed things because they did not know what else to do with them. She was quick and active, never still a moment. She was large, strong, and ruddy. She was very wilful. She "would or she wouldn't," and that was the end of it. Her parents had always left her to have her own way, and she ruled. This was a great hindrance to her teacher.

As the days went by, she became more and more eager to express herself. When she could not make herself understood, she would burst into fits of anger and would struggle and kick and scream and cry until she was worn out. These bursts of passion became more and more frequent—daily and even hourly. Dear reader, does it occur to you as you read this that you should be very thankful for your sight and hearing?

Helen's parents were much grieved over their little girl's sad condition. They wondered whether she could be taught.

By and by a teacher was secured who touched Helen's spirit and gave it sight. Thank God that a way has been found to teach the blind and deaf that converts their silent night to joyous day!

Helen's noble teacher, Miss Sullivan, came to Tuscumbia just three months before Helen was seven years old. She found that the two things she must first teach her wilful pupil were obedience and love. There were some hard struggles, but the teacher persevered, and in a letter to a friend she wrote, "The wild little creature of two weeks ago has been transformed into a gentle child."

Perhaps you wonder how Miss Sullivan could begin to teach Helen words since the child could neither hear the word spoken nor see it written. When she came, she gave Helen a doll and spelled in her hand (with deaf and dumb letters) d-o-l-l. Helen liked the finger play and she spelled the word, though she did not know that it was a word nor even that words existed. In the succeeding days she learned to spell a few other words.

One day she and her teacher were at the well-house, and as the cool water flowed over Helen's hand, Miss Sullivan spelled w-a-t-e-r. Somehow just then the mystery of language was opened to her. That word awakened her soul, "gave it light, hope, joy, set it free!" She left the well-house eager to learn, for she realized for the first time that everything had a name. She learned many new words that day, and when evening came it would have been hard to find a happier child.

Miss Sullivan did not have set times for recitation, but taught as the opportunity afforded itself. She and Helen strolled through the fields, the garden, the orchard, and a new world opened to the child, for she was taught about the sky, the sun, the rain, the growing plants, the birds, the animals; and she learned to love nature.

Helen was eager to learn and was very happy. She soon learned to read and to write. Only three months and a half after the first word was spelled in her hand she wrote a letter to her cousin. She used some large words and spelled them correctly.

When Helen was eight years old, she, accompanied by her teacher, went to far-away Boston to school. As she continued to learn and had new experiences, her world broadened and her avenues of happiness were increased.

BENJAMIN FRANKLIN—A SELF-MADE MAN

ON THE 17th of January, a little more than two centuries ago, Benjamin Franklin was born in Boston, Mass. He was the fifteenth child of a family of seventeen children. At an early age he showed such a fondness for books that his parents decided to educate him for the ministry. But after attending school two years, he was obliged to leave and assist his father in the business of candle-making. Benjamin, though disliking this kind of occupation, worked at it for two years, and in his twelfth year thought himself decidedly fortunate in being apprenticed to his brother, a printer. This business promised to afford better opportunities to study books, his one special desire.

After a time conditions arose which made his relations with his brother somewhat unpleasant. He determined to leave and start out in the world for himself. Consequently he sold some books and quietly left for New York. Finding no work there he set out for Philadelphia. When he landed in Philadelphia he had one silver dollar and one shilling in copper coin. He was only seventeen years of age, in a strange town, and four hundred miles from a friend. He soon found employment, however, with a printer, to whom he rendered himself invaluable by his skill and industry.

This was the beginning of a new and uncertain life for young Franklin, yet he had confidence in his ability to surmount any difficulties that he might encounter. Through the influence of a friend he went to England on a business trip which seemed quite promising, but on arrival he found that he had relied too much on promises which could not be fulfilled. He was obliged to secure employment to obtain money to pay his way back to America. After working in England about eighteen months, he returned to Philadelphia and found that the same printer for whom he worked before was willing to engage his services. So Franklin again went to work as a printer.

At the age of twenty-seven Franklin began the study of languages and soon became familiar with French, Italian, Spanish, and Latin. Besides these studies he read all the books that came within his reach. He had an ambition to obtain an education. He allowed no opportunity to escape unimproved. No matter how poor he was, he always managed to save a few pence with which to pay the loan on the books that he could not buy; no matter how hard he worked or how busy he was, he always found a few hours each week to read and study them. For two years he abstained from eating meat that he might reduce his board bill and thus save a little money to use in the improvement of his mind.

Franklin's grave

The efforts he put forth were not in vain. He gradually began to work his way into public activities. At the end of three years he was chosen postmaster of Philadelphia. Later he devised a plan for an academy, which was adopted and finally developed into the University of Pennsylvania. He also made some important

BENJAMIN FRANKLIN

electrical investigations. His discoveries have placed him in the ranks with the world's greatest discoverers.

In 1757 Franklin was sent to England as agent for Pennsylvania. There he associated with the greatest men of the time. And the poor journeyman printer of a few years before stood before kings and was honored by men of learning. In 1785 he was elected governor of Pennsylvania, which office he held for three successive years.

Franklin died in Philadelphia at the age of eighty-four. Numerous statues have been erected to his memory throughout the country.

Franklin stood among the most eminent men of the age, yet he was originally one of the most obscure of people. He raised himself to all this distinction almost without the aid of any education except such as he had acquired himself. Who will say, after reading this story, that anything more is necessary to the attainment of an education than the determination to attain it? Not all may have his natural ability; but all may imitate his industry, his perseverance, and his self-command.

THE PRINTER BOY

ABOUT the year 1725 an American boy, about nineteen years old, found himself in London, where he was under the necessity of earning his bread.

He was not like many young men in these days who wander about seeking work and "who are willing to do anything" because they know how to do nothing; but he had learned how to do something, and knew just where to go to find something to do. So he went straight to a printing-office and inquired if he could get employment.

"Where are you from?" inquired the foreman.

"America," was the answer.

"Ah," said the foreman, "from America! A lad from America seeking employment as a printer? Well, do you really understand the art of printing? Can you set type?"

The young man stepped to one of the cases, and in a brief space set up the following passage from the first chapter of John: "Nathaniel said unto him, Can there any good thing come out of Nazareth? Philip saith unto him, Come and see."

It was done so quickly, so accurately, and administered a delicate reproof so appropriate and powerful, that it at once gave him influence and standing with all in the office.

He worked diligently at his trade, refused to drink beer and strong drinks, saved his money, returned to America, became a printer, publisher, author, postmaster-general, member of Congress, signer of the Declaration of Independence, ambassador to royal courts, and finally died in Philadelphia, April 17, 1790, at the age of eighty-four, full of years and honors; and there are now more than a hundred and fifty counties, towns, and villages in America named after him. He was the author of "Poor Richard's Almanac." Who was he?

THE STORY OF A BUSY LIFE

THOMAS Alva Edison, known the world over as the "Wizard of Menlo Park," is indebted almost entirely to his own energy for all that he has achieved in life. A term of eight weeks in the district school marked the beginning and end of his school work. Happily he possessed a passion for reading, which, under the wise direction of his mother, made up for much that he missed through lack of school advantages. Before he had reached his twelfth birthday he had read Hume and Gibbon, and by his penny savings had become both owner and master of the whole edition of the "Penny Cyclopædia."

"But he was a genius," I hear some twelve-year-old boy argue, "and that accounts for his remarkable progress, both as boy and man." But what can genius do if kept rolled up in a napkin? Edison himself says of the success of genius, "Two per cent is genius, and ninety-eight per cent is hard work," and if he is mistaken in the compound, the error does not lie in rating the hard work proportion too highly.

Once a young man, who thought himself endowed above his fellows, declared, in Edison's presence, that "genius is inspiration."

"Nonsense!" exclaimed the "Wizard," "genius is not inspiration. Inspiration is perspiration." He had found this so in his laborious work.

Edison is not an expert mathematician, and rarely resorts to figuring in his calculations. He says he is not at all familiar with the multiplication table, and often has to count on his fingers when he gets into the sevens and nines. But, as everybody knows, he is at home when chemistry is introduced, and even in his boyhood devoured everything he could find on the subject with as much relish as other boys manifested for a story-book.

Edison began as a newsboy on the Grand Trunk Railroad. Making friends with the trainmen, the little newsboy improved his opportunity of examining for himself all the intricate and mysterious workings of the great locomotives. In his eagerness to make the most of his liberty, he established himself in an empty car, his aptitude for chemistry leading him to risk a miniature laboratory within his allotted space. An explosion of chemicals demolished his apparatus and, setting fire to the coach, brought the trainmen to the rescue, with the result that both boy and apparatus were thrown from the train by order of the irate conductor.

It was about this time that, risking his own life to save that of the little child of the station agent at Mount Clemens, Mich., the gratitude of the father took substantial shape in the offer he made to teach the lad telegraphy. Such rapid progress did Edison make that six months later he was appointed operator in the telegraph office at Port Huron. Though somewhat timid on account of his partial deafness, he proved a success in this first position, and from time to time, as occasion presented itself, was promoted to more responsible places.

The trouble with his hearing, a very annoying trouble, too, to one in his profession, was the result of one of those practical jokes that should never be played. When quite a small boy, Edison was standing on the station platform, watching the unloading of a heavy freight train. To frighten him, a brakeman, slipping up behind, caught him by the ears, and lifted him in the air, rupturing the drums of the delicate organs, an injury for which even the "Wizard" himself could invent no remedy; hence, though the greatest affliction of his life, he endures it patiently, thankful that his hearing was not entirely destroyed.

Two things are unknown to Edison—worry and discouragement. His most intimate friends contend that these happy characteristics are due to the fact that he possesses no nerves. Quite recently his secretary was compelled to report to him, in rapid succession, the absolute failure of three experiments, involving not only the loss of a pet invention, but also an enormous sum of money. Worn out with the strain upon his nerves, the young man was at a loss to account for the matter-of-fact way in which his chief accepted his report, and in an irritable tone asked, "How does it come that you take it so lightly, Mr. Edison? I should think you would be greatly worried over the loss."

"Why should I?" was the inventor's reply. "You're worrying enough for both of us."

Perhaps no man living possesses a greater number of medals and honor decorations than Edison. But so little account does he take of them that he is unable to tell for what many of them were given.

He refuses to talk into a phonograph, giving as a reason: "It would disgust me to see placarded on phonographs everywhere, 'Drop a nickel in the slot and hear Edison talk.' No, no; none of that for me! I'll not make a fool of myself there," and he did not, and nowhere else, either, so far as known.

Edison has one of the finest laboratories in the world, and not only is interested in his own devices and discoveries, but keeps up with the inventions of other men by subscribing to scores of scientific periodicals from all over the globe. The contents of these are translated for him by his librarians, and thus he is always abreast of the world's progress in science. But no other inventor, in any country, has a record quite like that of "The Wizard," and Edison deserves the title by a score of marvelous inventions.

A MISSIONARY TO THE RED MAN

IN APRIL, 1718, in the small village of Haddem, Conn., a little baby boy was born who was to become a great blessing and help to the red men, or Indians, of this country. You remember from reading your histories that at one time there were many more Indians living in this country than there are today and that they were not civilized as are those who live here now. Perhaps some of you have never seen a red man.

When this little boy was but nine years of age his father died, and five years later the death of his mother left him an orphan. For a time he made his living by working for a farmer, but a good minister, learning that he was very eager to go to school, asked him to come and live with him. This offer, David Brainerd, for he it is of whom this is written, gladly accepted; and he applied himself diligently to study. He spent three years in hard study with older ministers before starting out on his chosen life-work as a missionary among the Indians.

The young missionary of twenty-four went to work among the Stockbridge Indians in Massachusetts. He had a very hard time. The Indians were usually kind to him, but in the beginning the work moved slowly. The Dutch claimed the lands and threatened to drive the Indians away. They seemed to hate David for trying to teach the red men the way of life. At that time there was but one person who could speak English living near him. This person was a young Indian with seventeen letters in his name, which was far from being English. You may try to pronounce it if you care to. It was Wauwaumpequennaut. His first name was John.

Young Brainerd had no comfortable home, but he

A MISSIONARY TO THE RED MAN 153

stayed with a poor Scotchman, whose wife could hardly speak a word of English. His food was hasty pudding

A hill found to be an old Indian burial-place

(mush), boiled corn, bread baked in ashes, and sometimes a little meat or butter. No comfortable place was

154   BITS OF BIOGRAPHY

prepared for him to sleep, but he lay on a pile of straw in a log cabin, with the bare earth for a floor. This home

An old log cabin

was some distance from his beloved Indians, and almost daily he had to travel three miles on foot in all kinds of weather to be where he could teach them. He did not complain of his lot, but rejoiced in the presence of God and longed to "endure hardness as a good soldier."

A MISSIONARY TO THE RED MAN 155

Easier places were offered him, but he refused to accept them, choosing rather to endure sufferings and privations that he might bring the good tidings of salvation to his Indian friends. One day he wrote in his journal that he gave many thanks to God for His great goodness in allowing him to use more than one hundred pounds in New England money for charitable purposes during a period of a little more than a year. He said that he was thankful that he could be a steward to distribute what really belonged to God.

The exposure and hardship of these days brought illness and much suffering during his brief life. After two years his red brothers parted with him sorrowfully. He went to New Jersey, and from there to Delaware, where he began laboring among the Delaware Fork Indians. Here he took long rides on horseback, and many times spent all night in the woods, wrapped in his heavy coat and lying on the ground. His life was often in peril, but he toiled on. After a short stay with these Indians, he went to Crosswesung, N. J., and remained two years. Here he established a church and school.

His brave, heroic life, however, soon came to a close. It was said of him that he lived a long life in a very few years. At the age of twenty-nine he passed on to his great reward. Shortly before his death, Oct. 9, 1747, he said with his face aglow with light from heaven, "My work is done." He opened up a way for other missionaries to serve his Indians with less difficulty than he had experienced. The story of his life so influenced William Carey, Samuel Marsden, and Henry Martyn that they became missionaries, and through these Brainerd spoke to India, New Zealand, and Persia.

SUCCESS DESPITE MISFORTUNES

SOME men seem to choose a purpose, or profession in life; some seem to drift into it naturally; while others seem to fit into their place so well they can not get out. John Milton's great purpose in life, that of being a prophet to regenerate the social and religious life of his time, was no doubt inspired from the very spirit of the age.

He lived just at the time (1608-1674) when the Puritans were arising in England and when the Authorized Version of the Bible was first published (1611). The spirit of reform and religious sentiment seems to have been breathed upon him until he appeared to be driven or forced to perform the things that have so greatly enriched the world.

John Milton was born in London, and, excepting Shakespeare, became the greatest English poet. His first poems are rather light, and it was not until he was smitten with blindness that he planned and wrote his most wonderful books—"Paradise Lost" and "Paradise Regained."

In 1652 he became totally blind. Under this crushing gloom he gave to the world what is said to be the most pathetic sonnet in existence. It runs as follows:

> "When I consider how my light is spent
>   Ere half my days, in this dark world and wide,
>   And that one talent which is death to hide,
> Lodged with me useless, though my soul more bent
> To serve therewith my Maker, and present
>   My true account, lest He, returning, chide;
>   'Doth God exact day-labor, light denied?'
> I fondly ask: but Patience, to prevent
>   That murmur, soon replies, 'God doth not need—
> Either man's work or His own gifts; who best

SUCCESS DESPITE MISFORTUNES

> Bear His mild yoke, they serve Him best; His state
> Is kingly; thousands at his bidding speed,
> And post o'er land and ocean without rest;
> They also serve who only stand and wait.'"

As we carefully read these lines, we see how patiently he was learning to do God's will and to suffer that others might be enriched. It is true that he did not know how much his great poems were going to console and edify thousands and thousands of people; but God knew, and he could not make his work complete if he made his design known to Milton. God seemed to have a real purpose in life prepared for this great man. With courage and determination Milton followed in the humble line of duty, doing daily what he could amidst almost insurmountable difficulties until his great tasks were finished. He worked hard to accomplish what he considered only his duty, realizing that

> "All service ranks the same with God!
> There is no first or last."

He seemed to be impressed that it is not so much what we do as it is that we keep at the particular thing God wants us to do.

It is very noticeable, in reading the lives of various eminent men, that they pressed their way through obstacles of almost every conceivable form. Here was a man whose great purpose was to publish to the people the message of his soul. At the very time of life when his views were matured, he was overtaken by the very affliction that, from the general view, would ruin his work. He communed with God. He waited on God. God opened a way for him to express himself, and lo! his expression, his talent, is multiplied many fold by the very misfortune that befell him. His life would seem to say, "Through all obstacles continue to press on in duty's line."

TIMID CLARA'S GREAT SUCCESS

ON CHRISTMAS morning in the year 1821, there was born, on one of New England's lean hill farms, a baby girl who was destined to become an adopted child of the American nation. She was the founder of the American Red Cross Society; her name was Clara Barton.

She was the youngest, by twelve years, of a family of two boys and three girls; so upon her shoulders were shifted many duties too small for stronger muscles. "She brought home the cows, and milked, and wearied her small arms on the dash of the churn. She dropped potatoes, weeded onions, and picked the berries for pies."

Clara's parents and older brothers and sisters thought they must each have a part in little Clara's education, so one taught her mathematics, another taught her literature, another history and politics, and another horsemanship, etc., and these seeds of learning fell upon **fertile** soil. It is said she would waken her sisters before daylight on cold wintry mornings to help her find places on the map by the flickering flame of a tallow candle. Under such good tutorship she soon became advanced for her age. Of her first day in school she wrote later:

"I was seated on one of the low benches and sat very still. At length the majestic schoolmaster seated himself and, taking a primer, called the class of little ones to him. He pointed the letters to each. I named them all, and was asked to spell some little words, 'dog,' 'cat,' etc., whereupon I hesitatingly informed him I did not spell there.

" 'Where do you spell?'

TIMID CLARA'S GREAT SUCCESS

" 'I spell in "artichoke," ' that being the leading word in the three-syllable column in my speller."

The teacher smiled good naturedly and put her in the "artichoke" class for the remainder of the term.

But while yet a child, Clara became so timid she could not even tell her personal needs to her mother. Thinking to cure her of this, her parents sent her away to school. But there she was afraid of her schoolmates, of her teacher, and even afraid to eat. This so overcame her that she became dangerously ill and had to be sent home. She was examined, and the examiner stated that she would suffer wrong for herself but that for others she would be perfectly fearless. And this statement was soon tested. Her favorite brother became dangerously ill with a fever and for two years she nursed him so closely she almost forgot there was an outdoors. Stricken with grief at his misfortune, she would sit for hours at a time by his bedside. But at last he was nursed to health and the little girl, emerging from her state of seclusion, was more abashed than ever.

At the age of sixteen she began teaching, but the first day found her so abashed she had to fasten her eyes upon her Bible and read aloud for sometime before she was able to look the children in the face. But in the end she proved such a good disciplinarian that she received many invitations to teach. She forsook the teaching profession for head clerkship in the Patent Office at Washington, where she expected to clear up certain scandals she had heard of. She being the first woman employee in the department, the other clerks tried in many ungentlemanly ways to drive her out. But she held her ground, discharged some clerks, and instilled in the rest a new sense of honor.

Four years later in the same city there came to her

an opportunity that initiated her for her life-work. The Civil War was on, and one day while at the railway-station she saw a horde of muddy and mangled soldiers detrained. Among them she recognized some of her own friends and former pupils. Viewing the confused situation, she quietly donned an apron and began. She went from cot to cot binding up wounds and encouraging the discouraged. A few mornings later the postman handed her a great bundle of letters. From that time to the end of her life she found herself useful to her full capacity.

In times of war or in peace calamities, many people have been made to thank the ministering hands of Clara Barton. Her rule was to do the thing nearest at hand. In her own words she says: "I have never had a mission, but I have had more work than I could do lying around my feet, and I try hard to get it out of the way so as to go and do the next."